From Our House

From Our House

A Memoir

Lee Martin

A DUTTON BOOK

DUTTON
Published by the Penguin Group
Penguin Putnam Inc., 375 Hudson Street, New York, New York 10014, U.S.A.
Penguin Books Ltd, 27 Wrights Lane, London W8 5TZ, England
Penguin Books Australia Ltd, Ringwood, Victoria, Australia
Penguin Books Canada Ltd, 10 Alcorn Avenue,
Toronto, Ontario, Canada M4V 3B2
Penguin Books (N.Z.) Ltd, 182–190 Wairau Road, Auckland 10, New Zealand

Penguin Books Ltd, Registered Offices: Harmondsworth, Middlesex, England

First published by Dutton, a member of Penguin Putnam Inc.

First Printing, June, 2000
1   3   5   7   9   10   8   6   4   2

 REGISTERED TRADEMARK—MARCA REGISTRADA

LIBRARY OF CONGRESS CATALOGING-IN-PUBLICATION DATA
Martin, Lee.
From our house : a memoir / Lee Martin.
p.   cm.
ISBN 0-525-94546-6 (alk. paper)
1. Martin, Lee—Homes and haunts—Illinois.
2. Authors, American—20th century—Biography.
3. Martin, Lee—Childhood and youth.   4. Agriculture—
Accidents—Illinois.   5. Illinois—Social life and customs.
6. Fathers and sons—Illinois.   7. Rural families—
Illinois.   I. Title

PS3563.A724927   Z466   2000
813'.54—dc21
[B]   99-049707

Printed in the United States of America
Designed by Julian Hamer
Set in Adobe Garamond

This book is printed on acid-free paper. ∞

In memory of my mother and father

From Our House

O N E

My father, when he was a boy, took it upon himself to change his name. My grandparents had named him Leroy Martin, but when he went to school and started learning cursive handwriting, he had trouble forming a capital "L." His answer to the problem was to drop the first two letters of his name and become, from then on, "Roy." If he couldn't be "*the* King," he would settle for merely "King." So began his method for confronting obstacles with swift and decisive action.

One day, when I was a little over a year old, he was harvesting corn from a field he leased not far from our farm. It was late afternoon, November 3, 1956, and that evening he and my mother were supposed to go to my aunt and uncle's to watch the election returns on television. Everything I know about that day and the events beyond it I've had to piece together from bits of information various relatives have let slip over the years and from a few letters I found in a drawer not long after my father died.

I know that all our lives began to curve and change that day in the cornfield when the shucking box on the picker clogged, and my father tried to clear it without first shutting off the tractor. The picker, I would later learn from an old newspaper report, was a Wood Brothers corn picker with six "snapping rollers"—devices similar to the rollers of a wringer washing machine, only studded with hard rubber fingers. As the rollers turned, these fingers worked the corn on through the shucking box. On this day, a key on one of these fingers had sheared off, and the shucking box was filling up with corn. My father was raking the corn out of the box with his right hand when the rollers grabbed onto it and pulled it in.

There he was, one hand caught and one hand free, and a split second to decide. He reached in with his other hand, and the rollers caught it, too.

I'm free to imagine the day anyway I like: a brilliant sun glinting off the picker, the dry leaves of the cornstalks scraping together in the wind; or perhaps it was overcast, the sky dark with the threat of rain, and perhaps the wind was cold on my father's face.

We lived in a township where the farmland stretched on for miles between houses that sat far back from the roads down long, tree-lined lanes. It was a vast landscape of cornfields, soybean fields, wheat fields. On occasion, a cloud of dust would roll up as a car sped along the County Line Road that passed our lane, and my heart would quicken. I so desperately wanted the car to slow and turn down our lane because I was an only child, eager for company, and often a nuisance to my parents, who were too busy with work to entertain me. Sometimes, particularly during harvest season, weeks would pass and the only people I would see would be my mother and father and Grandma Martin who lived with us. I would start to imagine that the mouth of our lane had closed, the way it did in winter when the snows came, and that no one could reach us.

I suspect that my father feared that no one would ever find him that day in the cornfield. Fortunately, though, a gravel road ran by the side of the field, and finally another farmer driving past heard my father's shouts. I don't know how much time had passed, as my father stood there, the rollers mangling his hands, and I can't imagine what those minutes were like for him. I don't know what my mother was doing when the phone rang in our farmhouse, and she got the news. And when I try to think of myself on that day, it's nearly impossible. It's as if I didn't exist.

When my parents found out that my mother was pregnant with me, the first thing my father said to the doctor was, "Can you get rid of it?"

My mother was forty-five at the time, and when she stunned me with this story after my father had died, she explained that he had asked the doctor that question out of concern. Concern for her and a first pregnancy, obviously unplanned, so late in her life. I imagine all of that is true, but still I find myself searching for signs that they were glad for me.

I have my baby book in which my mother recorded the facts of my birth in her neat grade-school teacher's penmanship, joyful with crisp lines and looping curves. And I remember a toy-sized rubber motorcycle, saved for years, because it was the first gift my father bought for me after I was born. I also have a Christmas greeting card my parents had made in 1955 when I was nine weeks old. It's the size of a postcard, and there's a pencil drawing on one half of it. It's a drawing of a house, set back from the road, the peaks of its gables and the chimney of its fireplace rising up behind a snowbank. There's a picket fence out by the road and a beaming gaslight, and a gate with a Christmas wreath hanging on it. The gate is open and there are puddles of melting snow on the path that leads to the house. The caption reads:

Greetings . . .
from our house
to your house

My father, at the time, was riding the wave of Eisenhower prosperity. He owned his land and equipment; he had a wife and a son. So to the left of the Christmas scene on the card, there's a photograph of me. I'm wearing a shiny jumper, a short-sleeved white shirt, and a bow tie. My eyes are bright, my mouth is open in a smile, and I look as if I'm damned glad to see whoever's out there beyond the reach of the camera's lens. In fact, I look a little bit like Ike—that same bald head, that winning smile. We're in the middle of a booming decade, and I'm a jaunty ambassador, put on that card to let anyone who gets it know how happy I am in my home.

But, as the years go by, I learn that there are unhappy families all through our part of southern Illinois—families who live in poverty or with some other misery they try to hide. From time to time, I catch glimpses of their troubled lives. One of my schoolmates comes with his father to our farm to beg for work. An older boy kills his father with a shotgun blast. My family harbors its own secret, my father's temper, which he often turns against me. With his belt, he whips my buttocks, my legs, my arms—whatever part of me he can reach.

And I love him because he's the only father I have to love, and I think I must surely deserve his whippings because I'm a wicked child, too irritable, too stubborn, too full of sass. I don't know, then, that the moment in the cornfield has already determined years and years of anger between my father and me, or that such tensions are common between fathers and son. Instead, I rejoice in the few moments of closeness we share. On Sunday afternoons, he turns on the radio and I lie close to him on the couch, dozing to the sounds of a St. Louis Cardinals' baseball game. On Friday nights, I go with him to basketball games at the high school, and later we stop at a cafe for hamburgers and chocolate milk shakes.

He brags about my athletic abilities to his friends. "You should see him throw a baseball," he says. "I tell you he's got an arm."

The day of my father's accident, a surgeon amputated the right hand and the third, fourth, and fifth fingers of the left. Three days later, gangrene set in. This time, the surgeon had to make his cuts above my father's wrists: three inches above the right one and two inches above the left.

While my father was in the hospital, my Grandma Martin and I stayed with my Aunt Ruth and Uncle Don. My mother stayed at the hospital, dozing at night in a chair by my father's bed. Aunt Ruth was my father's sister, and years later she told me about those days and how she took me to the hospital waiting room to see my mother, but every time I screamed and cried and refused to let my mother hold me. "You were just a baby," Aunt Ruth said. "You didn't know what was happening. Your whole world got turned upside down. I guess you were scared. I guess we all were."

My father finally left the hospital, and he and my mother and my Grandma Martin and I went back to our farm. He had to wait nearly six months to go to Barnes Hospital in St. Louis where he would learn how to use a set of artificial hands. "Hooks," he called them, prongs of steel that curved like question marks at the ends of flesh-colored plastic holsters.

The time he spent at home from November of 1956 until April of 1957, as Aunt Ruth told me later, was more complicated than most people knew. To those who saw him outside our home, it must have seemed that he was managing his circumstances. One story I remember, although I'm not sure which relative told it, was one about my father driving his pickup truck to Ed White's general store. I can imagine the people in that store speaking of him with admiration after he had gone. "Roy Martin. Driving his pickup truck with his stumps—with his stumps, I tell you—now how about that?"

But all our lives have private truths, and the truth about my father was that after his accident he brought a deep and abiding rage into our home.

His letters from Barnes Hospital are written in a spidery scrawl, the way he must have written when he was a child who was willing to sacrifice the first two letters of his name. The individual characters are legible, and I can imagine my father working hard, the pen held between the prongs of his right hook, to make each one.

> *St. Louis, MO*
> *2:15 pm*
> *Tues Eve*
>
> *Dear Wife and all,*
> *Hope this finds everybody and everything O.K. I am O.K. I get good eats and plenty of them. I slept good last nite. It rained last nite. Looks like it might rain some more. Got my training through for the day. My arms are tired and haven't got a very good place to write. Hope you can make this out. My room mate has been very sick boy since I have been here. There are three of us amputee guys here now. Well my courage is picking up that I might get to come home some day. Goodbye.*
>
> *With lots of love and kisses,*
> *Roy*

I knew those hooks as intimately as I ever knew anything about my father. Thick bands made from rubber wrapped the bases of the steel prongs, and wires ran along the plastic holsters to a harness of canvas straps he wore across his back. When he contracted the muscles in his shoulders, the wires operated levers at the bases of the hooks. The levers stretched the rubber bands, and the steel prongs opened. I remember the weight of the contraption and the way my mother helped him out of it each night and draped the hooks over the back of a chair. He wore long, white cotton socks on his stumps to protect them inside the plastic holsters, but still, from time to time, he would get a blister, and my mother would have to rub salve on it. I remember the freckled stumps, and the seams at their ends where the surgeon had sutured the skin.

I have a newspaper clipping from the *St. Louis Post-Dispatch*, a photograph of my father and his doctor appearing at the Industrial Health Conference at Keil Auditorium. My father is wearing his hooks, and the doctor is holding up the left one. Its prongs are open, right in front of my father's face, so close he could reach up and grab his own nose. He looks a little scared, uncomfortable there in front of the camera. His right hook is reaching out toward the doctor's left hand as if he wants to take it.

> *St. Louis, MO*
> *2:00 pm*
> *Thurs Eve*
>
> *Dear Folks,*
> *Just got dinner ate and a few odd jobs done. We went over to Keil Auditorium about 11 o'clock and gave another demonstration.* St. Louis Post-Dispatch *took mine and Dr. Dayton's picture. So watch for my picture in the paper. Might not know who it is. Ha! Glad to receive your letter. Hope the gilt has good luck with her pigs. May be home this weekend to stay. Got a promise yesterday. If I do get loose, be home on bus. Tell Ma and Lee I am O.K.*
> *Bye,*
> *Roy*

And so he came home on the bus, and got a ride from town out to the farm, and walked into the house, and my mother turned and saw him there, with his hooks, her husband, the way she would know him the rest of his life.

When I look at photographs of my father before his accident, my eyes go immediately to his hands. I try to figure out whether they resemble my own, but I can never really decide. His appear to be smaller, his fingers shorter, but that may only be the perspective of the camera. All I can be certain of is the sadness that comes over me whenever I look at those photographs. I want to tell my father about the Election Day that's coming and that moment in the cornfield when the shucking box will clog. "Shut off the tractor," I want to tell him, but, of course, I can't. He's there in the photographs, and I'm here over forty years later, recalling the cold steel of his hooks and how one night, when I was a teenager, he pressed one of them to my throat and pinned me to the wall, and I swore that he would kill me.

T W O

My mother called my name: "Lee Roy Martin." She used her stern voice, the one that never seemed natural, even though she was a schoolteacher who from time to time had to use that voice with her third-graders. She was a demure woman, and, when she had to speak with anger or heat, it embarrassed her. "Lee Roy Martin," she said again. "Hush."

It was July, 1962, and I was six years old. I had just run into the shelter house where my mother and several other women were serving vegetable chowder, sandwiches, and desserts to the people who had gathered in the grove of oak trees across the road from the Berryville School for the annual Fox Chasers' Reunion. The fox chasers let their beagle hounds loose at night and then listened to their bays as they caught the scent and began to run. The chase was the sport, the fox never caught or harmed. It was supposed to be music, but, whenever I woke in the night and heard the dogs somewhere in the distance, their yawping always seemed such a mournful sound.

I was screaming. A group of older boys had told me that Santa Claus was in the woods.

He was riding a motorcycle, they said.

He had an axe, they said.

He was chopping off little kids' heads.

I tried to tell my mother all of this, but I only blubbered and bawled. I howled like the hounds outside in the grove. They strained against their collars, rattled the chains that leashed them to stakes driven into the ground. Their owners had drawn numbers on their sides with yellow paint so, if a dog were lost, it could always be returned. I clung to my mother, hid my face behind the folds of her apron. I heard another woman say, "Goodness, you'd think someone was murdering him." Then my mother, in a meek voice, said, "Kate, would you take us home?"

My father had brought us to the Fox Chasers' Reunion and then had gone back to our farm to cultivate his soybeans. I imagine he would have preferred to have been with us, sitting out under the oak trees, gabbing with the other farmers. There was a part of him that was generous and friendly and made him easy to like. Often, we would linger at the general store on Saturday nights so he could shoot the breeze with the other customers. Sometimes he would bring vegetables from our garden and give them to whoever wanted them. We would drive home in the dark, the night air, tangy with the scent of curing hay, rushing in through our truck's windows, and I would let my head fall across my father's lap, and I would go to sleep.

On this day, he had work to do, and while my mother and I were at the Fox Chasers' Reunion, I knew he was making pass after pass through the dusty bean field.

Miss Kate was my Sunday school teacher, and she led the singing at the Church of Christ, calling out the hymns in her monotone voice. She was a skinny woman with plain features—a long, narrow nose; thin lips; close-set eyes; ears with drooping lobes the size of men's thumbs. She wore metal-rimmed glasses that made her look even more severe, a hairnet, plain oxford shoes and white bobby sox. She was my mother's age, fifty-two, but unlike my mother, her girlhood friend, she had never married. What resentment she may have harbored because my mother had found love when she had not, I can only guess.

Miss Kate drove a Rambler the color of road dust, a box of a car with a square nose. She drove so slowly as we left the Fox Chasers' Reunion that I got the notion in my head that at any moment Santa Claus on his motorcycle would appear behind us, his axe glinting in the sun. That's when I leaned over the seat and shouted in Miss Kate's ear. I screamed out a line I must have picked up from television—*The Untouchables,* perhaps. "Can't this thing go any faster?" I yelled.

Ordinarily, in public, I was a meek, well-behaved child, but fear had driven me to lunacy. "Faster," I shouted.

And Miss Kate spoke in a voice that could barely contain the satisfaction it gave her to say these words to my mother: "What a bad boy. What a bad, bad boy."

At home, my father was in the field along our lane, and soon after Miss Kate had gone, he drove his tractor to the house to see why my mother and I had come back early.

"Something about Santa Claus and an axe," my mother said. "Some of the older boys teasing him, I suspect." We were sitting on the couch, and she had her arm around me. "I think this little boy is just tired. Too much excitement for one day. He's worn to a frazzle."

I started to cry again, in part because the boys had made me a fool and also because now, in front of my father, I was ashamed that I had been afraid in the first place.

"Little shits." He banged his hooks together. "Probably some of those fox chasers' boys. Someone ought to slit their bags and run their peckers through them."

I had always known my father to be a crude talker. Even his marriage to my mother, a woman who used no oath stronger than "fiddle," hadn't changed him. Nor had fatherhood. "Roy," my mother said, her voice low with warning, but, of course, it was too late. I had heard. *Slit your bag. Run your pecker through it.* That's what I would tell the next boy who lied to me.

"You should see those soybeans." My father stood at the screen door and looked off down the lane. The gentle roll of a hill, rose and levelled just past a thicket of blackberry briars and hickory trees, and there, stretching out to the horizon was the green of the soybean field, the plants ankle-high and just starting to claim a purchase in the clay soil my father had plowed and disked and harrowed. "Those goddamn dogs have been through there. They've trampled a swath." He turned and pointed a hook at me. "Now stop that bawling or I'll give you something to cry about."

My mother was rocking me, whispering in my ear. "Shh, shh, shh," she said, but the more I tried to stop, the more I cried. I was at the point I knew so well in childhood, that moment of panic where I believed everything was beyond me; the world was about to spin out of control. Santa Claus could come out of the woods on a motorcycle and behead me with an axe, or my father could reach for his belt and start whipping me.

Although he never really maimed me, he often left red marks on my skin, marks that faded more quickly than the heartache that filled me on these occasions. I was a sensitive child, and whenever my father whipped me, I imagined that he didn't love me, would never love me no matter how good I was. Perhaps if he had still had his hands and had only spanked me, I might have more readily forgiven him, but the fact that he could only use his belt made everything between us more ugly. I screamed and tried to leap away from the belt's lash, and my gyrations infuriated him. He chased me about the house, which was suddenly a place of chaos and not a home at all.

On this day, as I sat with my mother on the couch, I heard my father's belt buckle coming undone, and then saw him working to free the belt with the point of his hook. I howled. I tried to squirm away from my mother, but she held onto me. Each time my father went into a rage, I hoped that she would save me, but she never did. I was too young to know then that she was as helpless in my father's house as I.

"Stand away from him," he said, and though I tried to cling to her, she pried my arms from her waist.

The first lick of the belt was fire on my leg, as was the second and the third. I tried to move out of the way, but always the leather found me. All I could do was curl into a ball, try to make myself as small as I could, and wait for my father to tire.

Although there were times when things were sweet between my father and me, this was the touch I knew most intimately from him, never the feel of his skin on mine. I knew the cold steel of his hooks, the smooth plastic of the holsters into which he slipped his stumps, the rough canvas of the harness straps he wore across his back. Sometimes, when he had taken off the hooks, and they were draped across the back of a kitchen chair, I slipped my slender arms down into the holsters and tried to imagine what magic it took to make the hooks open. I could pry them apart with my hands. The underside of one prong was smooth; the other was rough with a grid of raised steel like the surface of a waffle iron or a meat pounder. I knew the sharp feel of the wires that ran along the side of the holsters, the thick rubber bands wrapped around the base of each hook. I never touched my father's stumps until I was older, but sometimes I brushed my fingers over the soft cotton arm socks he wore, the ones my mother safety-pinned to his tee-shirt sleeves. I was eager for him to touch me with this same tenderness.

For years, he had cut hogs, herded cattle, wrestled machinery. If he wanted to move a hog into the castrating chute, he hit it with a cane; if he wanted to bring a cow up a ramp to a livestock truck, he shocked it with a cattle prod. He was reckless with his hooks. He used them to hammer on rusted nuts, pry out cotter pins, stretch planter chains to their cogs. He no longer had hands; he had tools. Whatever resisted him, he forced to obey.

I lay on the couch a long, long time after he had gone back to the field and I let myself hate him for a while. As evening came, I heard my mother lighting burners on the gas stove, smelled the sulfur from the match. Soon my father's tractor sputtered and then went quiet as he pulled it into the machine shed. The leaves shivered on our maple trees. The light was softer now, and soon we were sitting at our table, the fluorescent ring burning overhead. Grandma Martin asked the blessing. Then my father said, "I'm give in for one day."

"Yes, it's been a long day," my mother said.

And we were all timid, waiting, as we always did after my father whipped me, for our world to return to normal.

The next day, Sunday, I went to church with my mother. She clipped a bow tie to the collar of my white shirt. She wet a comb and parted my hair. "Run get your Sunday school lesson," she said, and I did.

Outside, the locusts were chirring. All summer, I had found their brittle brown shells clinging to the trees, and I had marvelled again and again over how they had walked right out of their bodies and gone on.

My father was already in the field; the tractor's engine rumbled and then died away at the end of a row. The smoke stack clattered, and a squeal rose up as he held the left brake and swung the tractor around for another pass. I knew the dust was flying up around him, coating his boots and the olive green work suit he wore. I knew, when we finally came home from church, he would come to the house for dinner, and he would say, "I'm choked." My mother would pour a glass of iced tea and tell me to take it to him. I would hold the glass and wait for him to open his hook. I would try to figure out the exact moment to let the glass go, afraid that if I were too slow his pincers would clamp down on my fingers.

At church, Miss Kate said, "Well, I hope someone is in better spirits today."

"It was all the excitement," my mother said. "You know how little boys are. Full of imagination. Sometimes they get carried away."

I had learned in Sunday school that Jesus loved me. I had seen his face on the cardboard fans that the local funeral home provided, the ones that the people in church waved on those hot summer Sundays. He was descending from the clouds on a broad ray of sunlight. His arms were held out in welcome. My mother had read the caption to me: "For God So Loved the World." She had told me the story of how God had sent his son to save us all. Jesus had died and then had risen and had gone to prepare a place for us in Heaven. "Forever," my mother had said, but I had never been able to fathom it. What was forever to someone like me? I had a father in the here-and-now who, at my least provocation, could explode in anger. "Forever" was how long I waited for him to stop whipping me. It was nothing that led to Heaven.

"Jesus wants you to be good," my mother told me from time to time, and I promised myself I would try.

The Berryville Church of Christ was a one-room building covered with white clapboards, a red brick chimney rising from its peak. It sat off a gravel road on a plot of ground bordered by maple trees. In the summer, when the windows were propped up with the sawed off ends of broomsticks, I could hear the leaves stir. Sometimes I closed my eyes, laid my head over on my mother's lap, and listened to the drone of the preacher's voice, the whisper of the tissue-thin pages as someone thumbed through a Bible. I smelled the scent of my mother's powder, felt the steady rise and fall of her stomach as she breathed, and I was content, there in that place, where no one could hurt me.

My mother, I believe, felt the refuge, too. She had been the oldest in a family of six children—Beulah Abigail Read, the daughter of Maude and Harrison Read—and a good share of the parenting had fallen on her. "Boodie," my Uncle Jim had called her when he was younger even than I, because he hadn't been able to pronounce "Beulah." It seems such a severe name now for a young girl, but at the time my mother was born—1910—it was a name of comfort and mercy. My grandparents had named her after the idyllic land at the end of John Bunyan's *Pilgrim's Progress*, a land of rest.

It was peace we both found at the Church of Christ, relief from the strain of living with my father. My mother had never spanked me. She had rarely even raised her voice to me. I remember how she came in the middle of the night, when I woke, afraid of the dark, and how she sat with me until I went back to sleep.

I loved her most in summer when school came to an end, and she no longer left early each morning to make the drive to Claremont where she taught. She was with me all day, and there were never those awkward moments, as there were during the school year, when I was alone with my father—mornings as we waited for the school bus to pick me up, or at the end of the day when I came home, or on those days when I was sick with tonsillitis, drab winter days when the light failed early, and I stood at the door, looking down our lane, waiting for the soft glow of my mother's headlights. In the summer, the days were long, and my mother was always at hand. I woke to the churn of her wringer washing machine, listened to the wind popping the sheets she put out to dry on the line, the wooden clothes pins clicking together as she dropped them into her apron pocket. I played with my toy trucks in the dirt of the garden as she hilled potatoes, staked pea vines, snipped zinnias and marigolds. I smelled tomatoes cooking down to juice, heard the scrape of the colander as she culled out seeds and pulp. I listened to the snap of green beans as she broke them, the ping of hulled peas falling into a Pyrex bowl.

Each Sunday at church, after the members had taken communion—a piece of pie crust from a platter, a sip of grape juice from a goblet—we all marched to the front and dropped a bit of money into a straw basket. My mother always gave me a dime and held me up so I could reach the basket. On this Sunday, I saw a tarnished tin button, blending in with the quarters and dimes, and it gave me an odd feeling to know that someone had put it there, someone who walked among us, afraid to say they had nothing to give, afraid to speak their need, someone who wouldn't want the secret known, anymore than I would have wanted it known that I was a bad boy and sometimes my father whipped me. I looked at the button, and I knew I wouldn't say a word about it. If there were others who knew, I would enter into their conspiracy of silence. Shame was so easily come by, found in the most common things—a button in a straw basket—there in church where I had always thought I was safe.

At home, my father lay down for a nap after dinner, and he was asleep when a strange car came down our lane. It was a rich car— I could tell that—a sleek, black car with shiny chrome bumpers. It was a city man's car, too clean and bright to have been driven much over the dirt and gravel roads that crisscrossed our township. The feeling I got was that it was a car no one would want to drive down our lane unless he had to.

The man who got out of the car was wearing a short-sleeved white shirt and a red-and-blue-striped necktie clipped to the shirt with a gold bar. The fat end of the necktie furled up in the breeze. I was standing at the screen door with my mother, and I heard her take a quick breath, the way she did sometimes when she pricked her finger with a needle. "Leslie Feary," she said. Then she pushed open the screen door and, together, we stepped out onto the porch. She reached behind her and closed the front door; then she let the screen door close lightly against the frame. "We don't want to wake Daddy," she said. I stood in front of her and let her put her hands on my shoulders. She seemed to be bracing herself as Leslie Feary came up our walk.

We lived on the Lawrence County side of the County Line Road, and I went to Lukin School. My mother taught at Claremont in Richland County. I knew that Leslie Feary was the superintendent of schools, but what I didn't know was that he had come to ask my mother to resign her teaching position, or that she had been expecting this would happen sometime that summer.

Mr. Feary wanted my mother to step down because the school board felt she was too soft on discipline. Her pupils took advantage of her good heart. They were "rowdy," he said. "Unruly." And because she refused to make them "toe the line," the school board thought it wise that she not return.

"Yes, sir," she said, and though I was standing right in front of her, her voice, so quiet, sounded far away.

Mr. Feary squinted at her. "So it's done," he said. "You'll put it in writing. Make it official."

"Yes," she said, and then Mr. Feary got back in his sleek, black car and drove away.

My mother had taught school for over thirty years. She had first gotten her license in 1928, right after she graduated from high school, as was possible in those days when a teaching position didn't require a college degree. As a young woman, she had attended the university in the summers, and had then come home in the fall to start another school year in the classroom. For over thirty years, she had been surrounded with children, and I can't imagine that they didn't love her. Each year at Christmas, she brought home the gifts they had given her—the candies and handkerchiefs and head scarves. Each spring, they gave her photographs of themselves, wallet-sized black and white portraits that said SCHOOL DAYS along the bottom. She surely loved them in kind, her "kids," especially in those days when she had no child of her own, no husband, and no prospect of one. For years, her pupils had brightened her days, and if they were, at times, a bit rambunctious, well, who was she to hold them to account, so thankful she must have been for their bright faces, the way they clutched her hands on the playground at recess, their chirping voices when they wanted her to notice them on the swings or the seesaws or the slides. "Look at me, Miss Read. Look at me." Surely, she had given thanks for the very life of them, and now, without a fight, she was willing to let them go.

"I was afraid," she told me years later when we spoke of the day Leslie Feary came to ask for her resignation. "What if your father had woke up and found him there? I would have agreed to anything to stop what I suspect would have happened then."

And when my father finally found out, as, of course, he had to, he said, "I ought to go find that sonofabitch. That gutless pantywaist sonofabitch. I ought to hunt him down and rip him a new asshole."

I wanted him to do that. I wanted to see his rage turned against someone other than me. Then I saw that my mother was crying. She was standing by the window, smoothing the folds of the drapes by running her fingers down their creases, and suddenly I was ashamed of myself for thinking what I had. I would spend the rest of my life balanced on the thin line between my father's brutality and my mother's compassion. "What would it look like if you were to hurt him?" she said. "What good would it do?"

And, for once, my father, like the person who had dropped the button into the offering basket, was quiet.

That fall, at school, there was a boy named David Sidebottom. He lived on the Gilead Church Road in a house that had sat empty for years, a house his parents had rented even though the clapboards had long ago lost their paint, and the window and door frames were crumbly with dry rot. "I doubt they've much got a pot to piss in," my father said once as we drove past. "Sidebottom, what kind of name is that?"

My father, despite his gruffness and his hot temper, was a friendly man, who liked nothing more than to go to town on Saturday nights and spend a few hours loafing at the barber shop or the pool hall. There were times on our drives to town when he would sing the old hymn, *Rescue the Perishing,* and he would surprise me with his reverent voice, his earnest plea for salvation. He was, for the most part, a generous man who was quick to offer help to anyone who needed it. I had seen him drive grain trucks for farmers who were behind with their harvest, stop to pick up hitchhikers—strange and dangerous looking men he didn't know from Adam—give odd jobs to someone down on his luck even though my father could have done the work himself.

But after the Sunday when Leslie Feary came to our house, and my mother resigned her teaching position, my father became suspicious and niggardly. Each time he turned down our lane, he kept an eye out for unfamiliar tire tracks. He got out of our truck from time to time and squatted in the dust to study the pattern of the tread. There were Gypsies about, he said, thieves who would rob us blind, and Lord knew, he kept reminding us, we didn't have much to spare, now that my mother had quit teaching.

David Sidebottom was dark-skinned with high cheek bones

and jet black hair. "Goodness," our teacher, Mrs. Watts, said the first time she saw him. "You're a little Indian."

Mrs. Watts was a plain-faced woman who rarely smiled. She was afraid, I imagine, that if she did, she would call attention to her thin lips, her knobby chin, her fleshy cheeks. Her eyes were her best features—clear and blue—and she used them most often to pierce a misbehaving student with a cold stare. But there were times, when they would open wider, and then the light would get in, and they would sparkle, and for a moment, Mrs. Watts would look pretty.

Our school was a two-room school. Mrs. Watts taught grades one through four, giving each grade her attention at certain times during the day. She would have grade four gathered around her at the front of the room for their social studies lesson while the rest of us stayed at our desks, working on arithmetic or reading or language arts. There were perhaps fifteen of us, country kids, who, for the most part, had been brought up to behave well. But still we were kids, and because Mrs. Watts couldn't watch over all of us at once, there were plenty of opportunities for mischief.

We sat at double desks, and the person who shared mine was a girl named Becky Lewis. Even though I was an earnest boy, generally timid and eager to please—and even though I secretly loved Becky—one day, I stabbed her in the hand with my pencil. To this day, I don't know why I did it. We had merely been doing our work at our desk, and her hand had been there, palm up, and, without provocation, I had stabbed it. Becky began to howl, and Mrs. Watts came out from behind her desk. We had turned into hooligans, she said. She shook her finger at me. Her nails were clipped straight across like a man's. "Even you, Lee Martin. I'm surprised at you. You've always been a little gentleman." From then on, she told us, we were going to operate under the Old Testament law of an eye for an eye; whatever someone did to us, we would do to them in return. "Would you want Becky to stab you with her pencil?" she asked me. I lowered my head and shook it. "Of course you wouldn't, and I expect the rest of you feel the same. So think about it before you act up. Put yourself in the other person's moccasins."

That evening, toward dusk, David Sidebottom's father drove their old Dodge down our lane. One of the rear fenders was rusted through, and the ragged edges shimmied and squealed—the frayed metal rubbing together. My father had just shut off his tractor, and he sat there while Mr. Sidebottom got out of the Dodge, leaving the door open so the dome light's glow fell across David who was sitting in the front seat. I could see that his nose was running, and he was swiping at it with his sleeve. I was standing on the tractor's draw bar, my fingers gripping the rear rim of the seat. I peered out around my father and saw Mr. Sidebottom tip back his straw fedora. The point of the crown was split, and I could see a crack in the right lens of his eyeglasses.

"I was thinking I might be able to help you with the corn," he said to my father. Behind us, a field stretched back to the tree line. The dry stalks, heavy with ears, scraped together in the wind. "I can drive a tractor. I know how to run a picker. Or, I can haul loads to the elevator. Whatever you want. And the boy there, the boy can pick up loose ears from the rows. We'll do you a good job. The two of us." He turned back to the Dodge and called to David. "Come out here and say, 'pleased to meet you,' to Mr. Martin."

But David only sat there, his head bowed, wishing, I imagine now, that he wasn't in the light, where I could stare at him from my perch on the tractor. We knew, even then, that there was a world of difference between us. My father owned eighty acres of farmland, and though we had found ourselves tightening the purse strings after my mother had stopped teaching, there was still our farm and our house, everything paid for and in good shape.

"I'd like to help you out." My father took his foot off the clutch, and the tractor rolled forward a bit. Mr. Sidebottom stumbled as he took a quick step back toward the Dodge. "Really, I would. But the truth is, I can't afford to pay a hand this harvest. That's the long and the short of it, sad as it is to say."

Mr. Sidebottom got back in the Dodge. The springs creaked, and he had to slam the door four or five times before it finally latched. The points ground together as he tried to get the motor to turn over. Finally, it caught, and I heard the muffler rattle.

My mother came out of the house then, and the three of us watched the Dodge make its way back up our lane.

"What did Mr. Sidebottom want?" she said.

"Work," my father told her. "He was looking for work."

"And you told him?"

"I told him no."

My mother had a sweater tossed over her shoulders, held there with the top button fastened. "It would have been nice if you could have given him something."

"I know it," my father said, "but this winter, I've got to look out for us."

"Hard times always find the stumblebums."

"We're not like those people," my father said. He hammered his hook against the tractor's steering wheel, and the sound was sharp in the gathering dark. "By God, whatever we are, we're not like them."

The next day, at school, David Sidebottom kicked me in the shin. We were standing in the cloakroom, grabbing our coats so we could go outside for recess, when, without warning, he kicked me. He was wearing heavy brogans with hard, leather soles, and I cried out in pain.

"What's going on here?" Mrs. Watts came into the cloakroom. She had tied her head scarf beneath her chin, and somehow the scarf, the way it cowled her face, made her look even more severe than usual. "Mercy, what's all this to-do?"

"David kicked him," one of the older boys said, pointing his finger at me. "David kicked Lee in the leg."

"Is that true?" Mrs. Watts grabbed David by the arm and gave him a shake. "Did you kick Lee?"

"I kicked him," said David. He stared at me with his dark eyes.

"All right then," Mrs. Watts said. "All right. You know what this means."

She took us out of the cloakroom, and there in the hallway, she told me to kick David in the leg. "Go on," she said. "You know the rule."

I was wearing my P.F. Flyers sneakers, the ones that were all white and guaranteed, according to the advertisements, to make me "run faster and jump higher." I wished, then, that they could carry me far from that place because the last thing I wanted to do was to kick David. I had learned, from my father's whippings, that the worst pain from physical punishment wasn't the lash on the skin, but the bruise that blossomed and spread somewhere inside the soul. I thought of David, and how the evening before he hadn't been able to escape the glare of the dome light inside his father's Dodge. And now I couldn't avoid what Mrs. Watts and my school-mates expected me to do.

"Kick him," I heard a boy say.

"Yeah, let him have it," said another.

It was easy to dislike David. He was the new boy who wore ratty clothes, who always smelled of hot grease. He was stupid at his lessons, clumsy on the playground. He was everything none of us wanted to be. By the end of the school year, he and his family would move from Lukin Township, and I would think nothing of him until years later when he would reappear as a teenager, and I would remember this moment in the hallway of the two-room school, and I would wonder what else I could have done.

I kicked him, but not hard. I gave him a timid kick, and he didn't even flinch. "It's his shoes," someone said. "Tennis shoes. You can't hurt someone with tennis shoes."

The truth was I didn't want to hurt him. I knew what it was to be hurt; I knew he had learned it, too. I knew that the last thing he needed was for me to kick him. I stared into his eyes, looking for some sign that he understood I had tried to do him a kindness. For a moment, his face showed no expression. Then he laughed. He laughed and laughed, and I felt small and alone.

There were men, I was starting to understand, whom other men ridiculed and thought light in the balls. Men like Leslie Feary who knew nothing about physical work or the dangers of the farm. "Pencil pushers," I had heard my father call these men—bankers, insurance salesmen, lawyers—and when he said it, I knew what it meant: They didn't get their hands dirty. They wore white shirts and neckties and drove shiny new cars. You couldn't trust them. They might foreclose on your loan, deny your insurance claim, slap you with a lawsuit. The farmers in our township—along with the loggers, the oil-field roughnecks, the refinery workers—boasted about their strength, their backbone, their grit. I grew up hearing their stories. Dick Price got one hand caught in a picker and used his pocket knife to cut it off so he wouldn't have to stand there and bleed to death. And there was Bert McCoy and Glessie Provine; both of them had lost a hand each. I heard men telling these stories at the Berryville store, at the grain elevator in Parkersburg, at the barber shop in Sumner. I saw their blackened thumbnails, mashed by hammers, the splits in their skin, the calluses on their palms. I saw how they shut up when one of the "pencil pushers" walked in—it was as if they weren't even there. "You aren't one of us," their silence said. "You don't belong."

My father raised pigs, and in every litter there was a runt. At feeding time, the other pigs crowded him out. He would never put on enough weight to make him a profitable sell. On the market, he would never fetch a price that would make up for the cost of raising him. These were the pigs my father ended up knocking in the head with a sledgehammer so he could save money. What did it matter? They were all going to slaughter anyway. "This little piggy went to market—" My mother had taught me that game with my toes. "This little piggy stayed home. This little piggy had roast beef. This little piggy had none. And this little piggy went, 'Wee, wee, wee,' all the way home."

After the episode with David Sidebottom, I started to fear that I was the runt, the one who would never be strong enough, the scaredy-cat who would believe that Santa Claus rode a motorcycle and chopped off kids' heads. I would be a "pencil pusher," a "peckerwood," a "one-ball man." What I had heard my father and others say about so many of these men would turn out to be true about me.

That winter, when my mother didn't teach, my father sold a load of hogs even though he would have preferred to have fattened them a bit more and gotten a better price. He loaded them on a snowy day just before Christmas. He put the stock racks on the bed of the pickup truck, and my mother helped him drive the hogs up the ramp—six of them finally crowded into the space.

I sat in the cab between my father and mother, and as the truck started up our lane, I could hear the hogs squeal and grunt; I could feel their weight shift and bump against the back of the cab.

"They'll bring something," my father said, and it was clear that what he was really saying was, "they won't bring enough."

Though I don't remember any particular poverty that year, I do recall how careful my parents were with money. Our pantry shelves were lined with canned vegetables from our garden; our deep freeze was stacked high with cuts of beef from a cow my father had butchered. We didn't go hungry, and we had fuel oil for our stoves, and my father managed to feed the livestock. But there was rarely room for extras: no new clothes, no pop or candy when we went to the Berryville Store, no basketball games at the high school in Sumner, or hamburgers and chocolate malts afterwards at Tom's Cafe. And there, at Christmas, I had waited for my father to go to Ed White's store and bring home the paper sacks full of "goodies" like he always did—the hard candies, the chocolate drops, the peanuts, the tangerines. "We're a little thin," he kept saying. "I think we'll be all right, but Santa Claus might have a hard time finding us this year."

It was cold in the truck, the heater not yet having much of an effect. I kept my hands balled up in my coat pockets and hunched my shoulders so my collar came up around my face. My father had the ear tabs on his hat pulled down. My mother had a woolen head scarf tied under her chin. The scarf smelled like fuel oil from that fall when she had worn it while she had raked and burned our leaves.

After a few moments, it got cozy in the cab. The heater was blowing out warm air, and there was a gentle sway as my father steered in and out of the curves. He had a special spinner knob on the steering wheel. The gap at the base of his hook just before the two pincers met and curved to their points, fit over the knob, and he used it to turn the wheel. Down the road we went, our tires hissing through the snow that was now turning to slush. The windshield wipers beat a steady rhythm. It was nearly sixty miles to the stockyards in Fort Branch. I curled in close to my mother, and soon I was asleep.

When I woke, the truck was coming to a stop, and my mother was saying, "My word. What in the world?"

I opened my eyes and saw the men—there must have been at least a hundred of them—filling the road that led to the stock-yards. The chutes and ramps rose up behind the front gate, above the heads of the men who stood in the road, refusing to let my father pass. Along the road, there were fires burning in empty fuel oil drums. Some of the men carried axe handles. The snow was dusting their shoulders, the bills of their caps. They were shouting, and their breath was spilling out into the air in puffs of steam the way it did when our cattle bellowed and snorted in the barn lot on cold days.

"Strike," my father said. "It's a strike." And though I didn't know what that meant, I could tell from his hushed voice that it was something he hadn't planned on and that it embarrassed him to be caught in the middle of it. He let loose of the spinner knob, and we sat there, the truck idling.

One of the men came to our truck, and he tapped on my father's window with his axe handle. He was a man with a crooked nose, pushed over to the side, broken, perhaps, in a fight. He was wearing insulated coveralls, and he had the hood of a red sweat-shirt pulled up over his cap.

It took my father a while to roll down his window, working at it with his hook.

"You think you're going to sell some hogs, boss?" the man said, and I understood somehow that calling my father "boss" was an insult. It was obvious that the man and the others like him were the ones in control. "Is that the ticket?" he said. "You intend to give those scabs some business in there?"

"We came a long way," my father said. "My wife and my boy."

I had never heard him call me his "boy," and for a moment I felt as close to him as I ever had.

"Didn't you know about this strike?" The man placed a finger against the side of his nose, leaned over, and blew a gob of snot onto the fender of our truck. "Where the hell are you from?"

"No," my father said, "I didn't know."

I had never seen him cowed by any man, and I was embarrassed for him.

"You turn around now," the man told him. "You go on back. You don't want to take food off my table, do you?"

My father raised his hook to slip it over the spinner knob, and the man saw them, then, those hooks, and he got flustered, turned shy. "I didn't know," he said. "Neighbor, you must have been through some rough times."

I saw my father start to work the muscles in his jaw, like he was chewing on something, the way he always did whenever he was mad at me. "I've done all right," he said. "Don't you worry about that."

"Sure you have, neighbor. I bet you have." The man took a step away from our truck and pointed the axe handle toward the gate. "Tell you what. I'm in the Christmas spirit today. Go on. You drive on in there. You probably need to sell those hogs more than I need to stop you. Go on ahead." The man moved on down the road, waving his axe handle. "We're going to let him in," he shouted. "He ain't got no hands. What say we do him a good turn? He's a good boy."

My father sat there, staring straight ahead. He sat there while the men peeled back from the gate.

"Roy," my mother said, and her voice was kind. "We can turn around if you want to. We can go home."

My father used his arm to pull the gear shift lever into low. "No, you heard the man," he said. "It's almost Christmas."

Now I can imagine what it must have taken for my father to have driven past the men who had gone quiet, who cast quick peeks at us and then looked down at their feet or off to the horizon, not wanting to be caught staring at those hooks. They were quiet, thankful, perhaps, that they were whole men, and their silence only announced that my father was a handicap, a man other men could feel sorry for, men who didn't know his temper, a temper he had to stifle because he was a stranger, far from home, and it was almost Christmas, and he had to sell those hogs.

When we got back to Lukin Township and headed down the Sumner-Lancaster blacktop, my father stopped at Ed White's store. It was a long, wooden building with a tin-roofed shed coming out in an "L" at the back. There were two gasoline pumps out front, and a cement porch with a row of steps leading up to the door. The ice cream case was just inside that door, to the left, and the counter with its cash register was immediately to the right. Ed was standing there, a cigar stub in the corner of his mouth. "Come in, come in," he said. He was wearing a tan-colored work suit, but, unlike my father's olive one, it was clean and freshly pressed. "Looks like it's going to be a white Christmas." He stretched his mouth out into a grin. "You get it?" he said. "A *white* Christmas."

He had always been a jolly sort, a friend of my father's since they had been boys. It had been Ed who had promised that if my father, thirty-eight at the time, ever got married, he would buy him a set of silverware for a wedding present. He made good on his word. The silverware came in a wooden case with a red felt lining. It stayed on our pantry shelf for years, rarely touched, except for the times when I would open it and run my hand back and forth over the felt to see how it darkened and lightened as if blood ran and ebbed just below its surface.

"I get it," my father said. "You're a laugh a minute."

Ed looked out the window. I could see the snow coming down at a slant. The wind had picked up, and the Coca-Cola sign that hung from the porch roof was creaking as it lifted a bit and then fell, rocking and rocking.

"You got the stock racks on." Ed took the cigar stub out of his mouth and pointed it at our truck. "You been selling hogs?"

"That's right," my father said.

"You sell them in Fort Branch? I heard there was a strike down there."

"You got to know how to talk to people. That's all. Now, you got any Christmas candy in this store?"

There were cinnamon balls dusted with powdered sugar, and peanut brittle, and horehound drops. There were walnuts and pecans, Brazil nuts and pistachios. "And some of those," my father said, tapping on the glass of the candy case with the point of his hook. "And those, and those." I was standing close to him, and he glanced over at me and smiled. I got the idea, then, that after what had happened in Fort Branch—the strikers treating him as a charity case—he was glad to order Ed around, making him measure and scoop and fill up the paper sacks with our goodies, saying each time, "And what else?"

"Roy, that's enough," my mother finally said. It was clear that my father's extravagance embarrassed her. "Ed's going to think we're throwing our money to the moon."

My father had a saying in those days, used most often whenever I made an excuse for why I had done a chore poorly or hadn't done it at all: "If 'ifs' and 'buts' was candies and nuts, we'd all have a merry Christmas." He didn't look at my mother. He kept staring into the candy case. "And those," he said. "And those."

The bell on the front door jingled, and I felt cold air swirl about my legs. I turned toward the front of the store, and there, coming down the aisle toward the candy counter, was Leslie Feary. He was wearing a long wool overcoat and rubber galoshes, the kind with buckles. He squeaked and jangled, and then stood still a moment, looking at my mother and father and me, at the line of paper sacks on top of the counter.

"My goodness," he finally said. "It looks like someone has a sweet tooth."

There was the sharp edge of judgment in his voice, and I imagine that what he was thinking was that it was true about my mother; that she couldn't maintain order in a classroom, couldn't say no to a child; there was the proof, those sacks and sacks of candies and fruits and nuts.

My father straightened. He turned around and faced Mr. Feary. "I guess a man can buy whatever he can pay for," he said. "Is there a law against it?"

"No, there's no law." Mr. Feary tapped his feet together to knock snow from his galoshes, and I thought of Dorothy clicking her heels so she could get home from Oz. "I need some gasoline," he said to Ed. "High-test."

"Hold your horses," my father said. "I'm still doing business here."

"We're almost done," said my mother. "Aren't we, Roy? Aren't we almost ready to go home?"

My father's jaw muscles were working again. "Maybe not. Maybe I'm just getting started." He tapped his hook on the glass again and told Ed to give him another pound of those chocolate drops and a half-pound of pistachios. Ed added two more paper sacks to those he had already filled.

Mr. Feary lifted the cuff of his overcoat and looked at his wrist watch. It had a face the size of a half-dollar and a stretchy gold band. "I'm late for an appointment," he said. He reached out and tapped my father on the shoulder. "Why don't you be a good neighbor and let Mr. White see to that gasoline for me."

That's when my father turned, the pincers of his hook already open. He jammed them into Mr. Feary's crotch, backed him up against the pop cooler, and held him there.

"You think your time's more important than the next guy's?" my father said. "You think the sun rises and sets in your asshole?" I knew how Mr. Feary must have felt, sorry that he hadn't kept quiet. "You're breeding a scab on your ass," my father always warned me whenever I started to misbehave. Now Mr. Feary had pushed him too far, and he was standing there, the pincers of my father's hook open around his balls. "Well, let's see how long we can wait," my father said, "before my arm gets tired and this hook snaps shut."

Ed came out from behind the counter. "Roy," he said to my father, and he tried to keep his voice cheery. "You don't want to do that."

"Roy," my mother said, and she said it like a prayer.

"If you hurt me," Mr. Feary said, "I'll have you arrested."

"Maybe you ought to hire me to teach school for you." My father was so close to him the bill of his cap touched the brim of Mr. Feary's fedora. "Maybe that's what you ought to do. Get someone like me who wouldn't be afraid to crack down."

"Maybe you should just back away now," Mr. Feary said in a small, calm voice, and it was clear that my father had gotten himself into a jam—"between a rock and a hard place," he would have said. He could maim Mr. Feary and pay the price, or he could step back, his threat so much hot air. "You're just popping off," he told me from time to time. "You're just talking to hear yourself roar." Either way, he would be a fool.

Despite his hot temper, my father was a rational man who didn't want to hurt someone and maybe go to jail for it. He stood there in Ed White's store, surrounded by the warm air from the coal-burning stove and the smells of shelled corn and wheat chaff, which always seemed to linger from the harvest seasons. I had seen him spend hours there, shooting the breeze with whoever was on hand to listen, the way he did at the Berryville Store, the grain elevator, the Fox Chasers' Reunion. I imagine that he meant to live a good and decent life, and for the most part, he succeeded.

I moved up close to Mr. Feary. "My dad will slit your bag," I said. "He'll run your pecker through it."

And that was when my father backed away, his behavior made all the more despicable by what I had said.

My mother stepped forward, took me by the arm, and pulled me to her. "I'm sorry," she said to Mr. Feary. "I'm sorry for my son."

We paid for the candy and the fruit and the nuts.

"You don't have to," Ed said. "I can put back whatever you don't want."

My father wouldn't look at him, and though I was only a child, I somehow understood that there was shame for us now in that store and in the township that lay covered with snow.

There was shame in the fact that Mr. Feary was pumping his own gasoline, already having given Ed a five-dollar bill. And when we finally left the store, there was shame in the paper sacks we carried, in the scents of the chocolate drops, and the dusty aroma of the peanut shells, and the sweet tang of the oranges and tangerines.

My father drove down the Gilead Church Road, steering with care because it was growing dark, and the snow was deep.

There were no lights at the Sidebottoms' house, but as my father turned into the short driveway, I saw, in our headlight's swath, the thin trail of smoke rising from their chimney.

"I figure we can spare some of this," my father said.

He waited in the truck while my mother and I carried several of the paper sacks to the Sidebottoms' door. My mother knocked on the oval glass. There was plastic sheeting tacked over it, and when I peered in, I could see the watery-looking flames of the logs that were burning in the fireplace. My mother tried the doorknob, and it turned. She pushed open the door, just a crack, just enough so we could set the paper sacks inside, and I felt the warmth from the fireplace. I imagined that the Sidebottoms had just gone on a short trip somewhere and now were caught in the snow, trying to get home. I imagined them opening the door and finding the paper sacks. They would open them, marvel over their grand fortune. They would stand in the soft glow of the firelight and wonder what good, what kind people had found them.

"Quick," my mother said. "We're letting in the cold." She closed the door, and we floundered through the snow. We bent our bodies against the wind. "Hurry," she said, as if we were thieves, anxious to flee before we were caught.

THREE

On Christmas morning, my Aunt Lucille, my father's other sister, came for my Grandma Martin to take her to Lawrenceville to visit her brother, my great-uncle, John. My mother and father and I spent the day at my Grandma Read's with my mother's side of the family. Everyone brought a covered dish, and we sat down to a feast. There was a turkey and a ham and bowls of mashed potatoes, noodles, green beans, dressing, gravy. There were elaborate Jell-O molds and fruit salads and desserts: pumpkin, apple, and mincemeat pies; angel food, chiffon, and red velvet cakes. The smell of coffee perking filled the house. The windows steamed over from the heat of the food.

After we had eaten, the men retired to the living room where they told funny stories. The women stayed in the kitchen, lingering at the table. Soon, the kitchen filled with the merry clack of dishes and silverware being washed and stacked, and the lilt of my aunts' bright laughter. The Reads were, in comparison to the Martins, a fun-loving bunch, and on Christmas, in their company, I was happy. Their high spirits were contagious. Even my father caught them, and he laughed as loudly as anyone. He had even worn his festive argyle socks, the ones patterned with red and green diamonds. "Ho, ho, ho," he kept saying to my cousins. "Did

Santy Claus find you?" At one point, after the women had started to come into the living room, I crawled up on my father's lap, and he said he had a joke for me, a knock-knock joke. "You start it off," he said.

I loved knock-knock jokes, so with great enthusiasm, I said, "Knock-knock."

"Who's there?" he asked me.

There was a moment when I didn't realize what was happening, and even as everyone started to laugh and I knew he had tricked me, it was still great fun, all of us laughing together.

My Grandma Read said to me, "He's being a dirty bird, isn't he?" I nodded. "Knock-knock," I said again.

"Who's there?" my father answered.

"Dirty Bird," I said.

"Dirty Bird who?"

"Dirty Bird you," I said, and everyone laughed again.

My Grandma Read had always been my favorite grandmother because she was kind and soft-spoken. I had stayed with her before I was old enough for school, and she had pampered me with special treats: buckwheat pancakes and maple syrup, butter and strawberry preserve sandwiches. In the afternoons, we lay down for our naps. I still recall the warmth of her body next to mine beneath the quilt on cold winter days. Outside, icicles hung over the eaves, and snow drifted across the yard. Inside, the heat from the oil stove warmed us. Even if I couldn't sleep, I was content to lie there, listening to the ticking of the cuckoo clock. I loved to see the doors open and the bird spring out to sound the hour.

When we left Grandma Read's on Christmas, it was late, and out across the dusk we could see light displays at farmhouses: yellow stars atop grain silos, eaves lined with red and green bulbs. I was content to listen to my parents talking in soft voices, laughing again about something someone had said. Beside me on the back-seat were the presents we had received: a flashlight for my father, a box of handkerchiefs for my mother, a toy truck for me. There was a silver bow on the truck, and it sparkled. I closed my eyes and imagined the snow and ice melting, and the world turning green with spring, and then the bright, glorious days of summer.

Our farmhouse was a box house with a living room and a kitchen and two bedrooms. My Grandma Martin had the front bedroom, and my parents had the one in the rear. I slept on a hide-a-bed in the living room, and sometimes my mother slept with me because I was afraid of the dark. The nights she and I lay side by side on the hide-a-bed, I felt safe, beyond my father's reach, and I imagined that someday we might leave him.

Each morning, my mother dressed him. She pulled white cotton arm socks over his stumps and safety-pinned them to his shirt-sleeves. She helped him into the canvas harness that held his hooks. He slipped his stumps into the flesh-colored plastic holsters. He rolled his shoulders to settle the canvas straps across his back. He stretched out his arms and opened each hook to make sure the system of wires and bands was working. Though he continued to farm our eighty acres, he relied on my mother to help him. I remember her crawling under a combine to grease its fittings, hefting sacks of seed corn to fill the planter boxes, using needle-nosed pliers to cut the teeth of baby pigs.

The way her life had turned out surely must have surprised her. It was so much more than she had expected, and, too, so much more than she had bargained to shoulder. She was an old-maid schoolteacher when my father found her. She was forty-one years old, still living at home in the house catty-cornered from the Berry-ville Store, which my grandparents leased. Wednesday evenings, when the store was open until nine o'clock, my mother separated the cream from the milk the farmers brought to sell. My father helped her carry the heavy cans to the storage cooler.

Perhaps it was on one of those nights, there in the cool air, the smell of sweet milk all around them, that he first started to woo her. Quite possibly, he came right to the point.

"Look here," he might have said. "I'm alone, and you're alone, and if you wouldn't mind giving me a whirl, I wouldn't either."

Or maybe he was shy because this was before he lost his hands and became mean. Maybe he said, "You teach at Claremont, don't you? I see you there sometimes at the basketball games. Some night maybe—that is if you've got the time to spare—we could go over to the cafe and have a milkshake."

Either way, if my mother hesitated, who could blame her. By then, she must have given up on finding love, and now here was this man, Roy Martin, who in many ways was so different from what she must have wanted. He smoked cigars and chewed to-bacco, and he could cuss a blue streak. She was gentle and soft-spoken. She read books and went to church and taught school. Why didn't he appall her? The only clue I have is a photograph of the two of them when my father still had his hands. They're stand-ing on the sidewalk in front of my uncle's house. My father has his arm draped over my mother's back; his hand clutches her shoul-der. There's a smug look on his face as if he knows he's just won the prize and wants the world to know it, too. My mother's smile is as sweet as any look I ever saw on her face, and it's clear she's proud that my father has claimed her. This is the time of their lives I can never know although, through the years, there would appear from time to time signs of the sweet man my father had surely been when he had won my mother. He would buy her a wrist-watch for Christmas and ask me to wrap it. "And don't forget the ribbon," he would say. "A shiny gold ribbon. That's her favorite."

On their twenty-fifth anniversary, he would give her a wall plaque, a painting of flowers with a sentimental message:

> *A little laughter,*
> *a little fun,*
> *brings happiness*
> *to everyone.*

Our house was my father's house, literally, since it had come to him, along with the eighty acres, through my great-grandfather, James Henry Martin, and my grandfather, George William; and emblematically, since it was my father who dictated the tenor of the life we lived there. Will Martin died in 1941, and by the time I came along, my grandmother, Stella, was old and nearly blind with cataracts. I remember her feeling her way carefully from room to room, her fingers brushing lightly over the walls, the door jambs, the kitchen counters. She was a tall, thin woman, and her blindness had caused her to emphasize her natural grace. My mother complemented this with a gentility of her own. When I think of the days we spent in that house, I remember her soft voice and the way she would sit at the kitchen table at night and mark her students' papers. I remember the pinkish-red blush of her marking pencil, and the elegant loops and lines of her handwriting. She read to me, taught me to do arithmetic, showed me how to rub a scrap of paper over the pictures I had colored to give the crayon a sheen. If not for my father and his demands, we might have lived a more gentle life.

One night, not long after Christmas, I irritated my father. I have long ago forgotten the circumstances, but I still recall vividly the harsh glare of the ceiling light in our living room, and how he became angry with me for some snit I had thrown. He lashed out at me with a yardstick and caught me on my legs, my wrists, as I hopped about, trying to avoid the blows.

When I recall this moment, the one person I can't place in the scene is my mother, although I'm fairly certain she was in the house, in the kitchen, perhaps, because the one detail I remember vividly is that my grandmother came from there with a cup of hot tea (surely my mother had made it for her). It was a hard, plastic cup, pink, with cracks along its brim. Steam rose from it in wisps. It must have been late, close to bedtime (perhaps I had been cranky about going to sleep) because I was wearing pajamas; and my father was in his T-shirt, his skin bare in the gaps between the sleeves and his arm socks; and my grandmother had braided her hair, it hung down her back in knots and swayed back and forth as she came toward the sound of my father's angry voice. "Are you going to stop that yowling? Do you want another lick?" How could I stop crying? How could I stop myself from screaming? "No," I usually shouted whenever I knew I had gone too far and caused my father to whip me. "No," I would say over and over, hoping that this one word could stop what was happening.

"Roy Martin," my grandmother said. "Leave that boy alone." Still the lashes came. "Roy Martin," she said again, but still my father wouldn't stop.

That's when she reached out. And somehow, through the cloud of her cataracts, she found the bare skin on my father's arm. She pressed the hot teacup into his flesh. "Goddamn it." He jumped back, and the yardstick fell from his hook. "You've scalded me."

My grandmother's voice was low and even. "I told you to stop whipping that boy."

Out of the people in our house, I never would have imagined that she would have been the one to save me—she was old and often sick and without the power of sight. But there she was with her teacup, the only force she had at hand, and she was willing to use it.

Deep down I only wanted to love my father and for him to love me. The fact that my grandmother, who could barely see, felt compelled to do what she could to stop his anger makes me sad for how far we could sometimes stray from love, and in a strange way, it draws me closer to these people who are now gone—my father, my grandmother, my mother—all of us held together, then and forever, by blood.

After that night, my father lost his fury for a while, became reserved, nearly shy, as if he were a child himself who had been caught misbehaving, and was trying now to walk the straight and narrow. I, too, was on my best behavior, ashamed that I had contributed to the moment that had required my grandmother to press her teacup into my father's arm. I had never felt particularly close to her until that night because she was so old and infirm, and at times severe like my father. I remember how she burned her toast each morning and stood at the sink, scraping the black away with a butter knife. I remember the rasp of her scraping and the acrid, carbon smell that filled our house. Because she was elderly and blind, she received government surplus food commodities from Old Age Assistance. Every other Saturday, we drove to Sumner to wait for the train that brought powdered milk, sorghum, peanut butter. The train was always late, dreadfully late, and I was always bored and whiny, frazzled from the long wait in the heat, the tedious hours spent with old men and women, all of them clutching their bushel baskets, their cardboard boxes, all of us in a limbo I blamed on my grandmother merely because she was old.

Then she saved me, and I began to feel a fondness for her. Some days, when she didn't feel well enough to get out of bed, I sat with her, and she told me stories about my father when he was a boy, about how he walked through our woods to the West Point School. "Goodness, yes, your father was a West Point man," she said, with a laugh, and though I didn't understand the joke, I laughed along with her.

One day, she told me to fetch a shoe box from her wardrobe. Inside the box were the valentine cards my father had saved from his school days. They were from Sarah and Billy and Lyle and Floe, from Lola and Melvin and Metta and Edward. Some of them had verses as messages: "This heart I've saved for little you/Don't say you didn't want me to." Or, "You stole my heart/so give me thine/And be my faithful valentine." But the one that interested me most was a card that was made from two paper hearts glued together at the top so you could lift the points and look inside. There was a picture of a horse glued to the outside of the card. On the inside was a picture of a hog, and below it, written in some kid's scrawl, was the message, "You're a pig." The card was from someone named Mariain.

"A pig," I said to my father when he came into the room to see how my grandmother was feeling. I scrunched my nose up and made an oinking sound. "Why did Mariain call you a pig?"

He looked at the valentines laid out on the quilt. "Those old things," he said. "They're ancient history."

"Oh, you remember Mariain," my grandmother said. "He was the one who threw your cap on top of the schoolhouse."

"I remember," said my father. He bowed his head, then lifted his eyes and gave me a timid glance. "Ma, I don't know why you're telling those old tales."

I'm not sure, that I was aware, then, of anything out of the ordinary having happened, but now, when I recall that moment, I suspect that my father didn't want me to know anything about him as a boy. But the fact that he had saved all those valentines, even the one that was insulting, touches me now in a profound way, makes him seem more human to me, a skinny kid with big ears.

One of the valentines had a drawing of a Gypsy girl inside a red heart. She wore a double loop of beads around her neck; golden rings dangled from her ears. Her cheeks were rosy with rouge; her black hair curled out from under the yellow scarf she had put over her head and tied in a knot at the side.

> *In foreign lands with Gypsy bands*
> *I've wandered the whole world o'er*
> *But back to you*
> *With a heart that's true*
> *I lay it at your door*

That day, the verse was, of course, too difficult for me to read, but still I knew the girl was a Gypsy girl because I had heard my grandmother talk about the days when Gypsy caravans had roamed the county's roads, had even camped in our woods. The Gypsies would come to the farmhouses and offer to sell their woven baskets, tinker pots and pans, doctor animals, trade horses, tell fortunes. No one could trust them, my grandmother said. They would steal whatever they could make off with, even babies. They had no homes and spent their lives tramping about, one step in front of trouble. "We'll give you to the Gypsies," my father told me from time to time, just to remind me to keep my nose clean.

I knew he was teasing because my mother always said, in a hushed voice, "Roy, you'll give him nightmares." Still, a fear of loss moved into me, and remains to this day, the fear that at any moment the people I love can abandon me, vanish without a word of warning, throw my cap on the roof, call me a pig, leave me to a Gypsy band sneaking off into the night.

There were times, those days on our farm, when my world

seemed safe and knowable: our yard squared off and enclosed with its wire fencing, and a gate that swung open at the front walk. That spring, the two maple trees—one in front and one to the side of our house—began to leaf out, and all summer they sent their winged seeds tumbling to the ground. The snowball and lilac bushes in our backyard bloomed, and my mother set out her marigolds and zinnias. Sometimes I sat in my Grandma Martin's room where the green curtains lifted away from the window with the breeze. I heard quail calling. "Bob-white," they whistled. "Bob-white." My mother's spade rang out at a merry clip as it sliced and turned the soil. My father plowed the garden and showed me how to sow the seeds.

As summer came, he taught me how to hill potato vines, stake pole beans, blanch cauliflower by folding the leaves over the heads and fastening them with clothes pins. He lived by the seasons, knew the old signs. When apple blossoms appeared, it was time to plant melons and pumpkins and beans; when the white oak leaves were as big as squirrel ears, it was time to get the corn in the ground. He planted potatoes when the moon was dark, set out tomato plants during the first quarter. He swore that the first killing frost would come three months after the katydids began to chirp; if our chickens molted in August, we would have a hard winter. I rode with him on the tractor while he sowed soybeans, walked the fields in summer while the wheat turned golden, and the heads drooped, heavy with grain.

I knew the smell of the earth thawing, the sounds of peepers trilling in the night at our pond, the taste of a blade of grass, the cool air at dusk, the rumble of my father's tractor, the sweep of its headlights back and forth across the field. I knew the lay of our eighty acres: the long field that stretched back to the tree line, the creek we had to cross to reach the back forty. If we cut through the woods, as we often did when we hunted for mushrooms beneath the may apples, we came out into the cow pasture and skirted the bare spot where an oil company had drilled a dry hole. To the west of the pasture, a field spread to the County Line Road; to the north, lay our hog lot, the two ponds, and then the barnyard. When we passed through its gate, we were home. My great-grandfather had acquired the land in 1884, had given it over to my grandfather in 1919, who had then deeded it to my father in 1940, one year before my grandfather's death. Our part of southeastern Illinois had been surveyed and divided neatly into sections. We owned, according to the language of the deed, "The South Half (S 1/2) of the Northwest Quarter (NW 1/4) of Section 18, Township 2 North, Range 13 West, of the Second P.M. [Prime Meridian], containing eighty (80) acres, more or less." To me, it was nearly the world, and I didn't know, that spring and summer of 1963, that I was about to leave it.

The call came on a Sunday, when my mother and I were by the hickory tree in our lane. She was helping me learn to ride my first bicycle. We had taken off the training wheels, and she was beside me, steadying the bike, which I couldn't keep from wobbling. Then, I heard the screen door at our house creak open and bang shut with a slap. My father called out, "Long distance. Hey, it's long distance." He waved his arm over his head, and the steel of his hook flashed in the sunlight. "Long distance," he shouted again, and my mother let go of the bike and began to run.

In those days, a long distance telephone call was so rare it usu-ally meant disaster or extreme good fortune. In this case, the caller was a Mrs. Frank. She was the Superintendent of Schools in Oak Forest, Illinois, a southern suburb of Chicago, and she was call-ing to ask my mother to come there to interview for a teaching position.

Since the episode with Mr. Feary, my father had kept close to our farm, and when we had to go to town, he didn't loaf around the pool hall or the barber shop as he usually did. What I didn't know was that he had insisted that my mother register with a job placement service in Champaign, and now they had found her this position in Oak Forest.

"Chicago," my grandmother said when she heard the news. "Why would you want to go all the way up there?"

She sat in her rocking chair, her chin lifted, her hands gripping the arm rests. Our living room was dim from the shade of the maple tree, and I squinted my eyes until everything blurred. I tried to imagine what it was like for my grandmother to see only vague shapes and shadows. I was too young to realize yet what all this was going to mean to us. I thought about inventing a pair of glasses so strong they would give back my grandmother's sight.

"Fellow has to eat," my father said.

I closed my eyes completely and let the world become voices. First my grandmother's: "Can't Beulah teach school somewhere around here?"

And then my father's: "Maybe it'll do us all good to get out and see the world."

I heard the creak of my grandmother's rocker. "I won't live up there."

My father spoke more softly than I could ever remember hearing him. "No one's going to make you do that, Ma."

"You think I can live here by myself? An old blind woman?"

"We'll work something out, Ma. There's Lucille or Ruth."

"Your sisters? I know what you're all up to. You're going to put me in an old folks' home."

"No one said anything about that, Ma."

"You better look at the deed to this place," my grandmother said. "I can't read it, but I remember what it says."

"The deed?" said my father. "I don't know what you're talking about."

"You do know." My grandmother's voice was fierce now, harsh enough to make me open my eyes. "You do, Roy Martin. Says you've got to let me live here. Got to take care of me. I don't remember all the fancy lawyer language, but I know what it means. Means you've got to see to me. Means you can't take my home away from me. You signed that deed; now you aim to go back on your word."

My father was standing by my grandmother's rocking chair. He reached out his hook and put it on her head, petting her ever so gently, with the curve of that hook. "You're making out like I'm some criminal." He gave a little laugh. "Like I'm Jesse James."

"It is a crime," my grandmother said, and though her voice was still fierce, I could see there were tears in her eyes. "A crime and a sin to toss your old mother away."

At that moment, a bird flew out of our stovepipe damper. This bird, a sparrow, swooped and rose, its wings batting against lamp shades, curtains, the ceiling, the wall. I ran to my mother, terrified, because I couldn't predict where the bird would go next. At times, it seemed to be coming straight toward me. Frantic, it twittered and cheeped, darted from corner to corner, scraped its wings across our windows. I started screaming.

"Keep him still," my father said.

"He's afraid," said my mother.

"It's a bird." My father banged his hooks together. "A goddamn sparrow. What's there to be afraid of?"

Finally, the bird landed a moment on our heating stove, and my father reached out with his hook, and clamped the sparrow around the neck.

Everything went quiet then. My father pushed the screen

door open and threw the bird out into the yard. He turned back to us. "There," he said. "Everyone happy now?"

My grandmother shook her head. "It's bad luck," she told us. "Terrible luck. If a bird goes out of the house any way but the one it came in."

That evening, we packed a suitcase for my grandmother and drove her to my Aunt Lucille's house. In the middle of the night, we left for Oak Forest. Like Gypsies, I thought. Like the criminals my grandmother swore we were. At first, our trip had sounded like a fine adventure. But once I knew my grandmother's fear—once I saw her cry at the thought that she would have to leave her home—I started to imagine that it was dangerous to get too far away from the place you knew best in the world. A few years before, I had travelled to Washington, D.C., on a train to see my Aunt Gladys, my mother's sister, who was dying of cancer. I had gotten sick in the twists and dips of the mountains in West Virginia; I had tried to play with a black girl, but her mother had yanked her by her arm, and said, "You leave off with that white boy"; I had roughhoused in my aunt and uncle's apartment, playing some sort of shoot-em-up with my toy gun, and my uncle had shouted, "Good Lord, this isn't the sticks." In the city, there were customs and habits I didn't know. As my father drove our Chevrolet over the country roads to the highway that would take us five hours north, I watched a miniature Coke bottle on the end of the key chain that hung from the ignition. It dangled and danced with each bounce and jolt, and if I let myself look at it just right, there in the glow from the dashboard, I could imagine it was a tiny boy, like Tom Thumb, kidnapped by thieves. I could imagine the boy was me.

We drove through the night, and the next morning it was raining so hard, my father had to pull off the highway and wait for the weather to clear. We sat in the parking lot of a hardware store, and through the rain sheeting down our windshield, I could see a sign—"Pittsburgh Paints"—the neon balls of red and blue and green fading behind the gray curtain of the rain. I imagined that was how the world looked to my grandmother—gray and watery—and I thought of her waiting for us to come home.

"Look at it come down," my father said. "It's raining like pouring piss out of a boot."

My mother had a road map spread out on her lap. "We're close," she said. "About twenty miles."

My father yawned. "Relax. We've got plenty of time."

I sat in the backseat, lulled by the sound of the rain and the fact that we were dry and warm there in the car. My mother took her compact from her purse and powdered her nose. My father sighed, and then he said, "After this lets up, we'll find someplace where we can get some breakfast."

"I don't want to be late." My mother snapped her compact shut. "You brought us all the way up here. You can at least make sure we get there on time."

I had rarely heard her use that tone of voice, and only once before with my father. The summer before, my cousin had accidentally hit me in the face with a baseball bat, and my mother, for a few days, had to lay a hot compress on my black eye. One night, late, I whined that the washcloth was too hot, and when she cooled it, I complained that it was too cold. "Can't you get it right?" my father said. He was standing in the kitchen in his T-shirt and boxer shorts, his stumps bare. My mother threw the washcloth down in the sink. "If the two of you don't like the way I do things," she said, "you can fend for yourself." She marched into the bedroom, and when she came out, she had a coat on over her nightgown and a pair of slippers on her feet. "Where do you think you're going?" my father asked. My mother started toward our back door. "I don't know," she said, and she was crying. "I'm just going." I ran to the door, pressed my back to it, and spread my arms just the way someone might do in a melodramatic movie. "No," I said. "I'll be good." My father's voice was urgent. "For Pete's sake, Beulah," he said, and my mother slowly unbuttoned her coat. She had won a small victory. She had made it clear how much both my father and I needed her.

I should have known, when she closed her compact and snapped at him, that she wasn't completely happy about his idea of leaving the farm for Oak Forest. Years later, after he was dead, she would tell me that we hadn't been in such dire straits as he had let on. We would have been all right had we stayed on the farm, but he had insisted that we make a move. "He thought we needed the money," she would tell me. "I think maybe he just wanted a change."

That day in the car, he ignored my mother's sharp tone. "We'll find a cafe," he said. "I might even have apple pie." He shifted his gaze to the rearview mirror and winked at me. "How's that sound? Apple pie for breakfast. I might even ask the waitress to put a scoop of ice cream on it. Apple pie à la mode."

It was clear that he was enjoying himself, and I imagine now that my mother was right; he was anxious for a change. I can only speculate on what had brought him to the point where he was willing to sacrifice the farm, lease out the ground and turn its management over to another man. What had happened to make him leave his home, his sisters, his mother? To leave all that space for the close living of the city? Maybe he was tired of responsibility, caring for the land, for his livestock, for my grandmother. Or maybe his run-in with Mr. Feary had shown him how violent he could be. Perhaps he thought it was dangerous to stay; perhaps he was ashamed. He had gone away from home once before in his life. In the 1930s, he had worked at Inland Steel in East Chicago. "Your dad and your granddad didn't always see eye-to-eye," my Aunt Ruth would tell me later. He had gone to East Chicago to prove that he could. Perhaps he was going north again to make it clear to Mr. Feary and the members of the school board that my mother could still teach, by God, and somewhere more sophisticated than their one-horse country school.

We got to my mother's interview on time, and while she was in the school, my father and I waited in the car. I went to sleep in the backseat, and, when I woke, my mother was back, and she was telling my father that she had met the principal, and the superintendent of schools, and the president of the school board, and that they had offered her the job. We spent that evening in a motel, and it was strange, the three of us together for the first time in a place that wasn't our home. The television set was broken, and my parents said there was no need to complain to the manager. I remember the great quiet that settled around us, none of us quite knowing what to do with ourselves. I stood at the window staring at a room catty-cornered from ours where the drapes were open enough for me to see images flickering on a television, some situation comedy where kids were sliding down a banister and their mother was standing at the front door prepared to hand out sack lunches.

The next day, we drove back to our farm, and late that afternoon, Aunt Lucille and Aunt Ruth brought my Grandma Martin home.

"Cut off your nose to spite your face," my Aunt Lucille said when my father told her we were moving to Oak Forest.

My parents and my aunts were in the living room, and I was with my grandmother in her bedroom. She asked me to help her recall the photographs she kept in a box alongside my father's mementos in her wardrobe. Perhaps she had taken me into her room so the grown-ups could be alone in the living room to discuss my father's plans. The photographs were on thick rectangles of cardboard like the flash cards my mother used to teach me arithmetic. They were so unlike the snapshots we had of me, the ones that came back on flimsy squares with scalloped borders and the month and year printed along the side. And in these portraits, the people were posing, not caught, unaware, in the middle of something. One man was standing by a cedar tree, but it was clear that the tree wasn't real. I could see a block of wood nailed to the tree, only partially hidden by the limbs. The man was resting his arm on that shelf in what was supposed to look like a casual pose.

"That's your grandfather," my grandmother said, after I had described the photograph. "That's Will Martin."

There was one of a young woman. "In a dress with a collar that comes up to her chin," I said.

"And ruffles on the sleeves, and a shiny satin bodice," said my grandmother. "That's me when I was a girl." I laid the photograph on her lap, and she ran her finger slowly over the slick surface as if by some chance she might feel the swell of those young lips, those smooth cheeks. "Find the ones of the babies," she finally said, and her voice was hushed.

I sorted through the photographs and found several portraits of babies. They all wore long linen gowns, white, with lace hems. "There's a bunch of them," I said.

"Find one propped up in a wicker chair." My grandmother was patient with me. "And one in a chair covered with fur."

I found them and took them to her. "Is one of them my dad?" I asked.

"The one on the fur is Owen," she told me, "and the other one is Lola. Do you remember on Decoration Day when we take flowers to the Gilead Cemetery?" I thought of the coffee cans wrapped in tin foil, the ones my mother filled with peonies and irises, to set on the family graves. "Two of those graves at Gilead are for Owen and Lola. They were my babies."

"What happened to them?" I asked.

"Colic. We kept our milk and butter in the ice house in those days, and sometimes in hot weather it turned a little. Those poor babies got sick. It wasn't out of the ordinary back then. Those poor babies. We called it 'summer complaint.' "

In the living room, my father's voice had risen to a point where we could no longer ignore it. "You think you can tell me what to do? Goddamn it to hell."

He was crying. "Listen to you bawl," my Aunt Lucille said.

And then there was a volley of shouts and sobs, my father and his two sisters, their voices filling our house with misery. They squawked and shrieked and screamed. Footsteps stomped over the floorboards. The damper lid rattled on our stovepipe.

My Aunt Lucille's voice rose above all the others, and in a language, then strange and mysterious to me, she said, "The grantors herein reserve to themselves and to each of them a life estate in the premises above described." Only now, as I read the clause of the deed by which my grandparents transferred ownership of the farm to my father, do I realize what my aunt was reading. "With the right to live thereon so long as either shall live."

I only knew, then, that my father and my aunts were mad, mad, mad.

"What about me?" he said. "You see these hooks? The hell with that deed. You see what this farm cost me?"

I heard his hook strike the stove, scrape along the wall, hammer against the door jamb. He pushed open our screen door and let it slam shut. I saw him pass the window, cross the yard to the garden, not even bothering to step over the squash and cucumber vines. "Step on one," he had always told me, "and you'll kill it." He disappeared into the cornfield, the green stalks rising now above his shoulders.

"Bawling like a baby," my Aunt Lucille said, but this time she said it in a hushed voice.

"Oh, honey." My Aunt Ruth's voice was a soft coo, and I knew somehow she was speaking to my mother. "Sometimes he's such a chore."

"Those poor babies." My grandmother rubbed her hands over the photographs of Owen and Lola, as everything went quiet in our house. She closed her eyes. She took her time. She let her fingers touch and touch and touch as if some heat in her skin might bring her babies back. "They just up and died."

FOUR

Over the rest of the summer, we made ready to leave our farm. My father sold his livestock. He leased our ground to a neighbor. We packed my grandmother's things and moved her to my Aunt Lucille's. Finally, on Labor Day weekend, we loaded our car and drove up our lane. I could feel autumn coming in the cool air. Soon the leaves would turn and then drop to the ground. I remembered the day my father had argued with my aunts and then stormed from the house. I had waited in the yard for him to return, venturing out from time to time to the edge of the garden. He had stayed gone for hours, coming back only when he was sure my aunts were gone. Now, as we left the farm for Oak Forest, I remembered what my Aunt Lucille had said about my father that day—"Bawling like a baby." I remembered thinking of him out there in the heat of the day, alone, walking his land.

On my first day of school at Kimberly Heights Elementary in Oak Forest, my third-grade teacher, Mrs. Langhout, sent me across the hall to my mother's room, also the third grade, to ask whether she had an extra geography book. It was a book that was familiar to me from my old school, a book called *Distant Lands and Their People*. My parents had agreed, when we had moved from the farm to Oak Forest, that my mother wouldn't be my teacher, although now I wished otherwise so on this first day there would be at least one face I knew.

I knocked on the door of my mother's classroom, and a girl with a bright red bow in her hair opened it.

"I'm supposed to talk to Mrs. Martin," I said to the girl, and it felt odd to say that, *Mrs. Martin,* when what I wanted to say was, *Mom.*

The girl stepped back, letting the door open wide, and the other students stared at me as if I were an alien creature.

I had noticed already that they spoke a different language. They said "soda" instead of "pop." They ate "dinner" in the evening instead of at noon, and "lunch" at midday instead of "dinner" as we had on the farm. Even when the words were familiar to me, they sounded strange. "Root" and "roof" were pronounced with the same short vowel sound as "soot"; "wash," which we had pronounced with an "r" in southern Illinois ("warsh"), went limp in the mouth, the short "a" sounding like it did in "wasp." Although I was in the same state, only five hours north of the farm I had always known as home, I might as well have been on another planet.

My mother came to the door. She was wearing a new dress, navy blue, with a thin belt, the same color, around her waist. I had helped her zip that dress that morning, and I had fastened the clasp of her beaded necklace. She depended on me for those favors because my father, although he was amazingly dexterous with his hooks, couldn't manage the delicate clasp of a necklace or the small tab of a zipper. I could do what he couldn't, and that gave me great satisfaction.

But now my mother acted as if she didn't know me. "Yes?" she said. "How can I help you?"

She must have felt as out of place as I did; she must have been as glad to see me as I was to see her. But somehow, because this new life felt strange to us, we were afraid to acknowledge each other.

"A geography book," I said in a quiet voice. "Mrs. Langhout said I was to ask you if you had an extra geography book."

"I'll have to look in the supply cabinet," my mother said. "Come with me, and we'll see what I can find."

The supply cabinet was in a corner at the rear of the room, and to get there we had to walk along the front where all my mother's students could stare at me. I was wearing a pair of new penny loafers, and I heard the leather squeak with each step I took. Finally, when my mother opened the cabinet door and our backs were to the class, she said in a whisper, "How's everything going?"

Later that year, I would learn about the Underground Railroad and how it had moved slaves to freedom in the north. At that moment, I felt the way I imagine anyone did who knew what it was to steal through the night, anxious to find a sympathetic face.

"Okay," I told my mother. I wanted to stay next to her as long as I could, shielded by the open cabinet door, but finally she handed me a book, and she shut the door, and there we were, once again in plain view.

I felt as though we were impostors. Impostors because we pretended to know the lives we were living. My father, more relaxed now that he was away from the farm, became a man of leisure. Each morning, he drove my mother and me to school, stopping first at Tony's Corner Store to buy a *Sun-Times*. He liked to take the newspaper to a cafe uptown where he had started to get to know the owner, and read the sports, and talk about the Cubs or the Sox or the Bears. He bought a hat to replace the cap he had always worn on the farm. The hat was a gray tweed, and it had a red feather in its band. The brim was narrow and difficult for my father to grasp with his hook. I imagine that unless my mother or I were around to help him off with it, he left his hat on, which probably pleased him because he was proud of it. In Oak Forest, he became a clotheshorse. He liked to go into the department stores and pick out sport coats and trousers, and from time to time a tie. He insisted that my mother buy dresses for herself, and shirts and pants for me. Though he never said as much, it was clear that he knew this was a different world. Gone were our overalls, our work boots, the plain cotton housedresses my mother had always worn.

The first few days, until the half of a duplex we had rented was ready for us, we lived in an apartment that our landlord kept for out-of-town guests. There was a white carpet in the apartment, and my father said we should all take off our shoes before we walked on it. He clasped the points of his hooks together and held them close to his stomach as he moved through the apartment, careful not to bump the glass-topped coffee table, the crystal-based lamps, the paintings with their gilt frames hanging on the walls. Along one wall, there was a mural, a painting of the ocean, its blue expanse seeming to stretch back to the horizon where an orange sun was setting. "Red at night," my father said, "sailor's delight." It was an old saying that promised fair weather ahead.

I remember how carefully we lived our lives even after we had moved into our duplex, the top story of a house on 153rd, just off Cicero Avenue. We used softer voices, knowing the family downstairs, the Lahrs, would hear us if we spoke out of turn. We knew they would hear us because sometimes we heard them.

One night, their son, Bob, began cursing his mother. "Goddamn it," he said. "You old witch. Goddamn it to hell."

I don't recall the source of Bob's anger, but I still remember how unsettling it was to listen to him rant and rave. It was, perhaps, the first time that I had been witness to another family's unseemly behavior, and I felt a deep and lasting shame because I sensed that in a way I was listening to myself, to all the times I had sassed my parents or thrown temper tantrums.

The Lahrs entered their half of the duplex through a door in the front; we used the back door and then climbed a flight of stairs to the upper half. I was sitting on those stairs the night I heard Bob Lahr cursing. Often, in the evenings, while my mother prepared our supper, I sat there with my transistor radio, listening to the deejay, Larry Lujack, count down the Silver Dollar Survey on WLS. I always sat where there was a crack between two steps in the stairway. Through it, I could see the light from the Lahrs' kitchen, could smell the food Mrs. Lahr cooked, could hear the clanging of pots and pans. On this night, I remember the smell of boiled cauliflower, and the sound of Mrs. Lahr's voice saying, "Oh, Bob. You don't want to talk like that to your mother." I could see shadows passing through the strip of light. "You don't know what I want," Bob said. "You don't know one goddamn thing about me."

Bob was in junior high, a raw-boned kid with blond hair cut into a flat top. Sometimes he let me shoot baskets with him or play touch football in the street. One day, I ran the wrong pass pattern, cutting in when Bob thought I was going to cut out, and he called me a stupid kid with his head up his ass, and I went home crying. I remember how angry it made my father. His jaw muscles clenched, he started down the stairs, only to be met by Bob coming to our door to apologize. "Ah, hell, Roy," he said to my father. "You know how it is. Sometimes you just go off half-cocked."

We did know how it was; we knew the heat of sharp words, the anguish of rage between people who, at heart, were supposed to love one another. Our living was full of desire and regret, yet when we went through our days, in the company of other people, we all pretended that wasn't the fact.

My mother opened our door and called to me in her soft voice. "Come inside," she said, and I went in to eat my supper.

Below us, the Lahrs' muffled voices flared from time to time, and I wished I was somewhere else, our farm, perhaps, where my father's rage and my own recalcitrance had known sufficient space to hold it secret from the world.

Often, on weekends, we drove back to the farm. We left after school on Friday afternoons. My father brought hamburgers and french fries and cokes from the cafe, and we ate as we drove. I remember how my mother fed him. She held up the sandwich so he could take a bite, lifted the paper cup of coke so he could drink through the straw. We sped along Route 49 in our Chevrolet, letting the cluster of the suburbs break out into open farmland. We drove through small towns where people much like the people we had been on the farm were shopping or taking in a movie or gathering at high schools for football games. We drove through Crescent City, Rankin, Cissna Park, Hunt, Hope. "Hope we make it," my father always said when we saw the sign for the latter, and we drove on into the dusk.

He drove with his left hook slipped over the special spinner knob on the steering wheel. He used his right hook to operate the gear shift lever. He had always been a good driver, proud of the fact that he had never received a traffic ticket, had never been in an accident.

One night, just outside St. Marie, a mere thirty miles from our farm, my father fell asleep, and our Chevy veered off the highway, the wheels bouncing over the rough shoulder as the car nosed down toward a ditch. I was lying in the backseat, and my school books slid from the ledge along the rear window and fell on me. My mother called out, "Roy, my word." And I felt the tilt of the car as it pitched down the slope.

My father woke, then, and somehow managed to bring the car back up the grade until we were level on the shoulder. He let the engine idle, and we sat there, amazed by how quickly we had slipped into danger.

"You could have killed us," my mother said.

"I just dozed off," said my father, and he was sheepish. "I sure didn't mean to do that."

Because he had no hands, he must have thought he had less room for error than other men. They could foul up and blame it on their own stupidity or haste, implying that if they had only known more or had taken their time, they could have done the task correctly. But for my father, no matter the cause of his slip-up, it would always appear that he had erred because his hooks had somehow hampered him. It made him less forgiving; it made him impatient. Each time I misbehaved, did he imagine I was trying to take advantage of his handicap?

I remember how carefully he pulled back onto the highway that night, how we rode in silence, agreeing, without saying a word, that we would never mention what had just taken place.

"We're all right," he finally said. "We're almost home."

I suppose to my father home was always the eighty acres he had decided to leave. Eventually, I would inherit his footloose ways and his eternal longing for return. I would live in Arkansas, Ohio, Tennessee, Nebraska, Virginia, and finally Texas. To this day, I still wake in the morning, those eighty acres as real to me as my name. The farm comes to me in dreams at night. No matter how distant I am from it—no matter that the house has caved in and gone to ruin, and another man owns the land—it is the one place in the world I can never leave. I imagine it was so for my father the six years we spent in Oak Forest. No matter the reasons that had made him flee, he was always anxious to come back to his farm.

* * *

That autumn, it was always dark when we finally came down the County Line Road. My father nosed the Chevy into our lane; then he got out and walked into the headlights' swath to see what tire tracks had been left in the dust or mud. Sometimes he got back in the car and followed a set of tracks down the lane to see how far someone had come. I remember how, at the dip in the lane by the hickory tree, our Chevy would climb the hill and the headlights would catch the glint of the wire fence around the yard and the Farm Bureau thermometer tacked to the wall just outside the front door. "They came this far," my father said one night, and it gave me an odd feeling to know that someone—trespassers— had been nosing around, surely with an evil intent.

I slept again on the hide-a-bed in the living room, and some nights, headlights shined through the window and woke me. I watched the lights creeping down our lane, coming only so far before they saw our car in the farm yard. Then they backed down the lane and sped off along the County Line Road.

We had taken precautions. We had put a dead bolt lock on the front door and a bolt on the door between the kitchen and the back porch, a security bolt that locked only from the inside when someone slid it into a hole drilled into the door frame.

One night, my mother forgot the key to the front door, and we had to break a pane of glass in a window on the back porch, reach in, and undo the security bolt.

"It's a hell of a thing," my father said, "when a man has to break into his own house."

My mother was shining a flashlight through the broken window. I could see the library table on the other side, and the white box of the refrigerator, the cook stove, the heating stove, the kitchen table with its oilcloth covering it. From all appearances, it looked as if people still lived there, but this was the place we had abandoned, and we stole in like thieves, come to claim what wasn't ours.

Each time we came back to the farm, it was painfully clear how guilty we were. We had deserted our dogs, a collie named Rover and a beagle named Music, but they stayed, relying on the bags of dog food we left open for them in the feedway of the barn. Eventually, Music would leave, but Rover would remain loyal to the end, bounding out to meet us with excited barks each time we came down the lane. He was a three-legged dog, having lost a front leg when my Uncle Mick Green accidently backed his Plymouth over it. Rover was my father's dog, both of them maimed.

I remember that Rover was afraid of thunder and lightning. When a storm came up, he whined at the back door until my father opened it. Where did he go, I wondered, when we weren't there to let him in the house? Every time a car came down the lane, did he think it was us, come home at last to stay?

Often, in winter, when we were coming back to the farm for the weekend, Aunt Ruth's husband, Don, or Aunt Lucille's husband, Mick, would light our fuel oil stoves so the house would be warm when we got there. Aunt Ruth and Uncle Don had once rented a farm just off State Highway 50. The Moorman place, they called it, because a Mr. Moorman owned it. He was an engineer in Chicago, and finally he decided to sell the farm, and my aunt and uncle had to leave it. Uncle Don became a housepainter. They rented a bungalow in Lawrenceville near the Texaco oil refinery, and the only farming they did was a small garden plot behind their garage; the only animal they owned was a black cocker spaniel named Snap. Whenever we visited, my cousin, Roger, let Snap off his leash, and the two of us tossed rocks out across the yard so Snap could run after them and bring them back to us.

Roger must have been at least thirty, then. He had almost died from fever when he was a boy, and since then he had been what some might have called "touched," though they would have been wrong. He had a sharp mind that retained dates and facts. He knew the birthdays, anniversaries, deaths of everyone in the family. Often, we sat in the glider beneath their oak trees and, as cars passed on the highway, he called out the make and model of each one. Sometimes he would sit and stare as if he had suddenly turned to stone; when he spoke, his voice was soft and slow. Sometimes when he laughed, he laughed too loudly. He was a frail man, tall and slim with stooped shoulders. My Aunt Ruth had saved him from the fever by giving him alcohol baths, and, after coming so close to losing him, she was always on the lookout for any sign that someone's health wasn't up to par. She kept a medical reference book at hand and was quick to diagnose and remedy ailments. "You look peaked," she might say. "Your blood's thin. You're not getting enough iron." When I was fifteen, she would notice my bulging eyeballs, my trembling fingers, and the swelling in my throat. "That boy's got too much thyroid," she would say, and off to the doctor I would go, resenting her just a tad because she had pointed out, with the virtue of the healthy, that I was unwell.

Although my Uncle Don was always kind to me, he was at heart a gruff man, made brittle, I imagine, by the disappointments he had suffered. He had never managed to be a landowner, had lost the Moorman place, and now spent his days painting other people's houses. How in the world could he have ever understood why my father had left our eighty acres for our duplex in Oak Forest, particularly when neither my mother nor I—possibly not even my father—could have explained it, outside the fact that my mother had lost her teaching position, and, so my father claimed, we needed the money.

Uncle Mick was a different sort of man from Don. Mick had grown up poor and ignorant. As far as I know, he never learned to read and the only thing he could write was his name. He had been too busy hiring out as farm labor when he was a boy to worry about school. He shucked corn, worked on threshing crews, pitched hay. Come winter, he trapped beaver and muskrat and mink, and sold the pelts. When he was still a teenager, he started driving trucks. He saved his money and managed to buy a piece of land, part of which happened to be sitting over deep wells of oil. Just like that, he was rich, at least better off than the rest of us, and though he never lorded his wealth, it was clear that he had fallen into the gravy. I remember driving past the tall, silver oil tanks in his field, and my father saying, "I wonder how many barrels a day Mr. Money Bags pulls in." But no one could hold Mick's fortune against him, not even my father, because Mick was the sort of man who would do anything he could to help a fellow out, and if anyone deserved a break in life, he was the man.

Still, I imagine that my father, whenever we came for our weekend visits, enjoyed displaying his hat with the feather in the brim, the thin, leather boots that zipped up the side, the tweed sport coats he wore, the wool sweater vests. He liked to tell Don and Mick how much he had to spend for a haircut in Oak Forest— three dollars, when the going rate at Tubby's Barber Shop in Sumner was seventy-five cents—and he liked to talk about how much a gallon of milk cost and a loaf of bread. Even though he said these things with a shake of his head, as if he were appalled by the extravagance, it strikes me now that what he was also pointing out was that we had moved up to a higher class of living and could afford to pay the price.

"That's just foolishness," my Grandma Martin always said. Each time I saw her sitting in a chair at my Aunt Ruth's or my Aunt Lucille's, she looked so lost, her dead eyes casting about as if they were trying to light on some familiar form. At least when she had lived in our farmhouse, she had been able to reach out and touch the shapes and angles she could remember from the days when she still had her sight. My father had taken that pleasure from her when he had moved us to Oak Forest. He had rousted her from her home despite the fact that he had agreed, when my grandparents had deeded the farm to him, that he would allow them to live there the rest of their lives. My aunts had tried to shame him into staying, particularly my Aunt Lucille who was a more forceful woman than Ruth, and though eventually everyone forgave him, I imagine there was always a small seed of resentment over the fact that he had gone back on his word and abandoned my grandmother.

I can imagine my Uncle Don lighting our fuel oil stoves and feeling like a lackey. I can imagine Ruth, wary of any sign that city living might be ruining us. "Goodness," she said once, "what do you do for fresh air?" And Roger? Surely, he catalogued the date of our escape; more than likely, though nearly thirty-five years have passed, he still remembers it.

My Uncle Don called us "city slickers"; my Uncle Mick teased me—"Have you been up there kissing on those colored gals?" One night, my Aunt Lucille said to my mother, "Beulah, your hands are getting soft." And my Grandma Martin said to my father, "You'll be sorry one of these days. You reap what you sow."

What none of them knew, since we never spoke of it, was that my father and I had become more civil toward each other since we had left the farm, and my mother, who had tolerated our warfare, was thankful for the change. Still, we were outsiders in Oak Forest and outcasts when we came back to the farm. Our leaving had passed a judgment on those who had stayed. Because of this separation, we were able to love one another in a way we had never before been able to manage.

I remember how sweet it was to wake those mornings and find my mother and father in the kitchen of our duplex talking in low voices, to feel the warmth of the gas furnace, to smell hot tea steeping and bacon frying, to hear the radio playing softly in the background, my father listening for the temperature and the day's forecast. "It's colder than a well-digger's ass," he often said that winter, and then my mother helped him on with his coat and hat, and he went downstairs to start our car so it would be warm for our trip to school. Each afternoon, he would be waiting to take us home. I had never seen him as cheerful, as even-tempered. He had a good word for everyone: the Lahrs, the owner of the cafe, the school custodian, the principal. He made friends at the filling station, the post office, the supermarket. The tellers at the bank knew him, as did the garbage collectors and the regular customers at the cafe. Everywhere we went, I heard people call out to him. "Roy," they said, "what'd you know?"

What he knew was the pride of a man taking care of his family. He drove us to PTA meetings, to the forest preserve for picnic lunches when the weather was good, to basketball games at the junior high, and as the years went on and my talents emerged, to my own basketball games, my band concerts, my science fairs. He had never had the chance to participate in activities such as these when he was a boy because he had been a country kid, bound to his chores on the farm. Now that the farm was over two hundred miles distant and under the care of a tenant, my father gave all his attention to my mother and me. He even started taking us to church in Crestwood, a small town close to Oak Forest. Although he never joined the congregation, I imagine my mother was thankful for those Sunday mornings when we sat together in our pew, the three of us in our bright, new clothes; the life we had lived on the farm, hidden from all who saw us.

The church at Crestwood was large, much larger than the Berryville Church of Christ I had attended with my mother. At Crestwood, there were rooms and rooms where Sunday school classes met, and the nave was so grand the preacher had to use a microphone. We always arrived toward the end of Sunday school, and we waited in the foyer until that part of the service had ended and we could go in for the worship.

Even then, as we stole quietly into the nave, I was aware that we were somehow less devout than those who had come earlier. My mother walked on her tip toes so her high heels would make no sound on the parquet floor. My father joined his hooks at their points and held them at his stomach, the way he had when he had carefully made his way through the lavish apartment where we had stayed those first few days in Oak Forest. "Break something," he had said then, "and they'll ship us back to the farm." I sat in the pew between them, glad to shrink into the space they left because I was shy, even more so than I had been when we had lived on the farm. Or maybe I was afraid that at any moment someone might denounce us. "Heathens," they might cry. My father had said it to me often enough those days on the farm. "You're a heathen," he would say, and I would feel, as I did when we sat in our pew at the Crestwood Church of Christ, that I was lost. I felt it when my mother reached for the New Testament in the rack on the pew in front of us while others were opening the thick, leather-covered Bibles they had brought from home. I felt it when the communion tray passed down our pew and my mother was the only one of us to sip from the grape juice that represented Christ's blood, to break off a meager crumb of the cracker that was an emblem of his body. And when the preacher issued the invitation to those who wanted to be born again—invited us to put on a new life—I feared that we didn't deserve the grace our move to Oak Forest had offered us. When we left the church, and the preacher and the elders shook our hands, took my father's hook without shame, and said, "We're so glad to see you," I understood that they had marked him as an infidel, someone they needed to save, and then the life we had managed seemed suspect to me.

One evening, two elders from the church came to our duplex.

One of them had a bald head and wore eyeglasses with black frames. The frames were too big for his face, and he kept adjusting them, pushing them up on his nose. His name was Mr. Browning, and he stopped a moment at the dining room table where I was practicing my penmanship, writing letters over and over on a lined tablet. "Well, now that looks fine," he said. He bent over to get a better look at the tablet, and he had to put his hands to the temples of his eyeglasses to keep them from sliding off his face. "That looks like a jim-dandy job."

In those days, my handwriting was small, as if it were afraid to announce itself. My mother had bought me the writing tablet with its thin blue lines marking the height for lower and upper case letters, and each evening she made me fill them. I wrote single letters over and over—lowercase "a's," "b's," and so on. I practiced the loops of capital "L's," the circles of "O's," the arcs of "C's." I wrote my name, making it bigger than it had ever been. "Good," my mother would say when she would check my work. "That's good." And it would make me happy that I had pleased her.

Her own handwriting was beautiful, a gathering of elegant curves and lines. One look at any word she had written, and a stranger would know that she was a woman of patience. She sat with me each night while I went to sleep; the weight of her on my bed was the most assuring presence I knew. And, if I woke in the night and called for her, she always came.

"I could make you some coffee?" she said to the elders that night, and her voice rose at the end like the tail of an "e," the inflection displaying her doubt that she should extend this offer. On the farm, she would have brought out glasses of Pepsi-Cola or iced tea, but in Oak Forest, she was still trying to suit herself to the ways of city life. My father had adapted more easily than she because the people there were for the most part brassy like him, and a timid, reserved woman like my mother easily shrank into the background. One night, she had gone with some of the other teachers from our school to the movie *My Fair Lady.* She came home with her coat smelling of cigarette smoke, and I tried to imagine her riding in the car, the other teachers puffing away, chattering on and on about the movie, while she sat in the back seat, nodding at their observations—*such singing, such dancing*—but offering no opinion of her own for fear it would seem ridiculous. "Or ice cream?" she said to the elders, again with that questioning tone. "We have vanilla ice cream?"

"Some coffee," Mr. Browning said. He straightened and patted me on the back. "That sounds jim-dandy."

The other elder had a Bible tucked under his arm. He was a bit younger than Mr. Browning. His name was Mr. Laycoax, and his thick eyebrows had grown together in a single line across his brow. "Nothing for me, thank you," he said, and he hoisted his Bible up more firmly beneath his arm.

My mother went into the kitchen, and my father and I were left alone with the elders. My father was sitting in the living room, and there was an awkward moment, after my mother had gone, when the elders seemed unsure whether they were to join him there or whether they should wait where they were until she returned with the coffee. My father said nothing to help them, and finally Mr. Browning said, "It's some weather we've been having, wouldn't you agree, Mr. Martin?"

It may have been the first time I had ever heard someone call my father Mr. Martin, and the odd sound of it made me sense that the elders had no particular affection for him. I realized, then, that the reason he wasn't inviting them to come into the living room and sit down, was because he didn't want them in our home.

"Colder than a well-digger's ass," he said, in a tight voice, and the elders glanced at each other.

Mr. Laycoax cleared his throat.

Mr. Browning pushed his eyeglasses up on his face and stared at my father. "I don't believe I've ever heard it put quite that way."

"It's just a saying," my father said.

"Indeed," said Mr. Laycoax. "Very quaint."

It was clear to me that Mr. Browning and Mr. Laycoax were different sort of men from my father; they had had more fortunate lives, and I suppose, in their presence, he must have felt the way my Uncle Don did—maybe even my Uncle Mick—when we went back home, and my father showed off his new clothes, spoke about the money he threw around. The world was full of lack and want, and all it took was the company of someone who thought he had a certain privilege to make that fact clear.

"I suppose you've come to save me," my father said.

"We've come for a chat," said Mr. Browning. "Mrs. Martin filled out one of our visitors' cards."

I imagined my mother writing our address in her precise and lovely hand and slipping the card into the rack at the end of our pew the way someone who was shipwrecked would fit a note into a bottle and send it out into the tide. How had she done it without my father knowing? Had she hidden a card in her coat pocket, taken it home, and returned it the next Sunday? Had she agonized over whether to do this, knowing, as she surely must have, that my father would resist any efforts to bring him into the fold?

She was a woman of eternal hope. She saw the best there was to see in people, and she had faith enough to believe that the worst would one day change. My father saw everything differently, and how could we really blame him? Since he had lost his hands, how could he keep himself from imagining that life, at any moment, could turn on him? How could he help but be on guard for betrayal and ruin? It seems a miracle to me, now, that he kept as much good will inside him as he did. And what stuns me is the fact that my mother, who must have been so thankful that he had finally started attending church, was willing to risk that victory on the chance that he might truly be saved. Like me, she must have been wary of the temporary change our life in Oak Forest had brought us. She must have longed for something more permanent. I had seen people accept the invitation in church, come to the front, crying, repenting of their sinful ways. I had seen the baptisms, had watched the penitent laid back into the water, and then brought up, some of them reaching their arms to Heaven, their lives fresh to them and new and without shame.

When my mother came from the kitchen, a tray held before her, she might as well have been offering her soul, so anxious she was for the elders' visit to go well. "I've brought coffee *and* ice cream," she said. Our best china cups, the ones with coils of pink flowers etched along the rims, rested on matching saucers; spoons rattled against dessert cups heaped with vanilla ice cream. "Surely, you've got time for both," she said, in a voice that was so bright it was hard to miss the desperation that charged it.

"Hot and cold," Mr. Laycoax said. "Fire and ice."

"That's Robert Frost," my mother said as she brought the tray into the living room and placed it on our coffee table. "I remember that poem from my college days." She cleared her throat and began to recite. " 'Some say the world will end in fire; Some say in ice.' " Then she stopped, and a sad look came over her face. "Well, mercy," she said. "Listen to me go on. Ice cream and coffee. What a silly combination. Help yourselves to the coffee, and I'll take the ice cream away."

"It doesn't matter," my father said.

"No?" said my mother.

"No." My father got up from the couch. I could see his jaw muscles, clenched, pulsing beneath his skin. He had narrowed his eyes into a squint, his brow pinching together into the worry line that would deepen as the years went on. "They aren't staying," he said, and he took a step toward the elders.

I had never known my father to turn a visitor from our home.

"We won't take but a minute," Mr. Browning said.

"I'm sure you have a minute," said Mr. Laycoax. He took the Bible from beneath his arm and waved it in the air. "To consider what Jesus says you need to do to save your soul."

My father tipped back his head and squinted at Mr. Laycoax. "I don't believe there's any saving. What's going to happen is going to happen. It's all been laid out, and there's nothing anyone can do about it."

"Like your hands, for example." Mr. Laycoax waved his own hand toward my father's hooks. "Nothing could have stopped you from losing them?"

I thought of how my father could have shut down the tractor and cleared the clogged shucking box in safety. "Lost is lost," he said. "Not even Jesus Christ himself can bring back my hands."

Mr. Browning smiled. "Maybe he can, friend. Maybe someday in Heaven. Think how glorious that would be. You wouldn't want your wife and son to be there without you, would you?"

At that moment, an angry voice rose from downstairs. Bob Lahr said, "Fuck you. Fuck you in spades." Then a door slammed, and I knew he had gone out into the cold night.

For a good while, no one said anything. Neither my father, nor my mother, nor the elders. From the table, where I still sat with my writing tablet, I could see Bob Lahr, his head bare, moving through the glow of the streetlight. The bristles of his flat top were white in the sheen. His hands were in his coat pockets, and he had hunched his shoulders to bring his collar up around his ears. He tromped through the snow; then he was away from the light and moving somewhere out of my vision along the dark street.

We would only be neighbors that one year, and though I would never mention the things I heard him say or ask him why he said them, when I remember him now, it is with a certain amount of recognition because he was the boy I would one day become—angry and cruel. In my mind, I can still see Bob Lahr, who screamed and cursed at his mother, and me, who listened from the stairs, hoping that the anger from below wouldn't rise through the cracks and return my father to rage.

The night the elders came, I listened to his voice filling with heat. "Save me?" he said. "Where was Jesus when I got my hands caught in that corn picker?"

"The Lord works in mysterious ways," Mr. Laycoax said. "Rarely is the reason for tragedy immediately clear."

"God gives us nothing we can't handle," said Mr. Browning.

My father's hooks banged together. "Listen," he said. "You don't want any of my religion, and I sure as hell don't want any of yours."

I thought of my Uncle Don and my Aunt Ruth, my Uncle Mick and my Aunt Lucille. They would never know what we had found in Oak Forest, a momentary stay against the rage that filled my father. If my cousin, Roger, had been present the night the elders came, surely he would have marked it as the moment that our mercy began to leave us. I sat at the table, my head bowed over my writing tablet. I concentrated on making the loops of the capital "L's" reach up to the highest blue line. With each motion of my hand, I recalled the way my Grandma Martin had traced her fingers over the walls, as she had moved through our house on the farm. My own fingers ached from gripping the pencil. "L," "L," "L," I wrote, the first letter of my name, wrote it again and again as if it were a code, a sign that would allow us to keep travelling through this land. "Red at night," my father had said the first time he had seen the sun in the mural at the landlord's swank apartment. Then, we had stood there—my mother and my father and I—in the midst of the landlord's fine lamps, his white carpet, his drapes—a long way from home, afraid to touch anything, afraid to move.

FIVE

One afternoon in our second winter in Oak Forest, my father got a call from Aunt Ruth who told him Grandma Martin was in the hospital. My mother's principal refused to let her leave school early, and, when we finally started the trip south, it was almost dark. The snow had started coming down, the second storm that week.

The snow banks along the highway were as tall as our car, and still the snow kept falling. The flakes, magnified in our headlights' glare, did a crazy dance. They came rushing at us, and, watching their swirl and dive, I got the feeling we weren't moving at all. But there was my father, working the steering wheel with his hooks. I could hear the squeak of his harness as he steered our car through the night. I could feel the scrape and whap of the icy ridges beneath the floorboards of our Chevy, and from time to time the rear of the car slid a bit and my mother reached out and braced herself by grabbing onto the dashboard.

"Don't go any faster than you have to," she said in a quiet voice, but it had been three hours since the call had come, and my father was in a hurry.

We were on Route 49 on a wicked night in February. We had gone through Crescent City and Cissna Park and Rankin, and now we were in the heavy snow and still more than a hundred miles to cover before we could get to the Memorial Hospital in Lawrenceville where an ambulance had taken my grandma because, as my Aunt Ruth had said, "her heart's give out."

Surely my father thought, then, as we made our way over the slick highway, of how far we had moved from the people who knew us and loved us best. Beneath my parents' remarks about the snow, I sensed their guilt and regret. Trouble had come, and now we were the prodigals trying to get home.

"If it would just let up," my father said.

"That doesn't seem likely," said my mother. "What a miserable night."

We drove into Ogden, and then, just as we were about to leave the town, traffic came to a halt. I saw the brake lights of the car in front of us go on, and then my father was easing down on his brake pedal, pumping it with a light touch so we could stop without sliding off the road.

A state trooper used his flashlight to tap on my father's window. The trooper stamped his feet, and I imagined how cold he was. My father was slow with the window. He kept bumping at the knob with the curve of his hook, and the window came down an inch at a time.

"Sir, I'm going to have to ask you to pull off the highway," the trooper said. He was wearing a hat like mine, a black, leather helmet with fur ear flaps and a strap that buckled under the chin. His eyebrows were icy with snow. "We're not letting anyone through unless they've got tire chains. Do you have any chains, sir?"

"No," my father said, "I don't have chains." He had always been proud of the fact that he had never been in an accident or received a traffic ticket. Even with his hooks, he was a good driver, and now he had to get us to Lawrenceville before he lost the chance to see his mother one last time. "It's like this," he said to the trooper. "My ma's in the hospital. We got the call a few hours ago." His voice cracked just a bit. "She won't make it through the night."

I was nine years old, too young to know that state troopers heard such stories all the time. I felt sorry for my father because he had to open our lives to this stranger, had to tell him we were too far from home at a time when we should have been close.

My mother leaned over toward the open window. She laid her hand on my father's shoulder, a tender gesture I had never seen her make, and I knew that she felt partly responsible for our predicament. If she hadn't lost her school in southern Illinois—if she had just been able to say "no" to her students—we wouldn't have moved to Oak Forest where her principal would say she couldn't leave school after the news came that my grandma was in the hospital, and my mother, even my father, would accept this verdict. It amazes me that my father, who had been so angry when Mr. Feary had fired my mother, that he had opened his hook and jammed it into his crotch, hadn't directed a similar rage toward the principal who had kept us in Oak Forest the last two hours of the school day. Perhaps my father was accepting his punishment for bringing us so far north. Perhaps he had felt guilty all along because he had left his mother for whom he had promised to provide. He had broken that promise, and that night in February perhaps he knew he was paying for it.

"He's a good driver," my mother said to the trooper in that soft, earnest voice that no one could mistrust.

The trooper bent over and took a closer look inside our car. I imagine him taking stock of my mother and father, both of them over fifty years old that night in 1965, and their son, whom they had never planned on having, sitting quietly in the backseat, his hands jammed into the pockets of his coat. We all must have looked so frightened, so shy, that our lying was out of the question. The trooper stepped back from our car. "Good luck," he said. "You're going to need it."

"I'll be careful," my father told him, and then we went on through the snow.

It was late when we got to Lawrenceville, so late that the parking lot at the hospital was empty except for my Uncle Don's pale blue Mercury idling near the entrance, exhaust fogging from its tailpipe. There was no snow here, only bitter cold. The asphalt of the parking lot had blanched white. The wind buffeted our car, and I heard the air whistle through the seals around our windows. We had crept over the icy highway, the snowflakes finally dwindling until we were out of the storm and driving beneath a clear sky, the stars thick and bright in their clusters. I recalled how often, when we had lived on the farm, we had driven through the countryside late at night, and a falling star had dropped from the sky, and my father had said that meant someone had just died. As we left the snow, and the sky cleared, I leaned my head back against the seat and watched out the rear window in case a star should fall and no one see it. But all I saw were the constellations twinkling, the Big Dipper and the Little Dipper with the North Star shining brightest at the end of the handle. So many times on the farm, I had gone out at dusk and waited for the first star to appear. "Star light, star bright," I had chanted. "First star I see tonight. I wish I may, I wish I might, have the wish I wish tonight." I had usually wished for something frivolous—a bicycle or a horse or a trip in an airplane. But on this night, when I knew my grandma was dying and my parents were ashamed of the distance that kept us from her, I wished that time could pass in a snap so we could be in the place where people were waiting for us.

And when we finally were, I saw the shadowy forms of my aunt and uncle and cousin through the windows of their Mercury. My Uncle Don and my cousin, Roger, were sitting in the front seat. My Aunt Ruth was barely visible in the back. Uncle Don had his hands on the steering wheel, as if he had been close to giving up on us and driving away. Roger was staring straight ahead, his lips pressed together. When we had finally parked beside them, it was my Aunt Ruth who rolled down her window. My mother rolled down hers, and my Aunt Ruth said, "Mom's gone." Her breath fogged out into the air. She was crying just a little, and she pressed a handkerchief to her mouth. "Two hours ago," she said. "Poor soul. She just couldn't hold on."

My father let his hooks fall from the steering wheel, and I saw his shoulders slump. I thought how weary he must have been, having driven so far over such treacherous roads. My Uncle Don was eyeing our car. When we would finally leave it, I would see the gray film of road salt, the frozen slush caking the fender wells, the ledge of snow on the roof.

"Looks like you've been through it," my Uncle Don said.

"Two hours," said my father. "That's what we had to wait until Beulah could leave school. Her principal wouldn't let her go."

"That's not right," Aunt Ruth said, and there wasn't a word of argument we could offer against her claim. "I'd think you'd just pick up and go," she said. "Stubborn the way you are."

Years later, after my father was dead, Aunt Ruth told me how he had never seen eye to eye with my grandfather. "They were both mule-headed," she said. "Oh, how they went round and round." That was all she told me, and I didn't have to ask for more details because by that time I had come to understand how tempers could take a father and son to the point where they could say hateful things to each other, where violence could become their regular come and go. What were the issues between us? They seem trivial now. The length of my hair; my inability to do a chore to his satis-faction, or my refusal to do it at all; my desire to sleep late in the mornings, a sloth he wouldn't allow; the typical teenage rebellions of cigarettes, alcohol, late nights. At heart, I suppose the problem between us was the same as it had been between my father and my grandfather—two generations of the same blood, each convinced that it knew how life was best to be lived.

In the 1930s, when my father was a young man, he left his fa-ther's farm for a time and moved in with my Aunt Lucille and Un-cle Mick in Hammond, Indiana. Mick was working in a steel mill in East Chicago, and he got my father hired on there, too. Years later, I would listen to the two of them tell stories from those days. My father always told one about a Puerto Rican boy who slit an-other man's throat with the lid from a tin can. "That's how rough it was up there in those steel mills," he would say. He would wait for some sort of reaction from his audience, and, if he got none, he would draw his hook across his own throat and add, "Yes sir, sliced his gullet, just like he was gutting a fish."

I never knew my Grandpa Martin—he was dead long before I was born—but I can imagine how he must have felt about my fa-ther going north, the same thing my Grandma thought in 1963 when we moved to Oak Forest. It was foolishness, a wild hair, at the worst an out and out betrayal. Will Martin was, after all, the man who, when he finally deeded the farm to my father, insisted on a clause that required my father to provide a domicile on the land for my grandparents as long as either should live. Perhaps my father's flight to the steel mills had convinced my grandfather that his son wasn't to be trusted, which turned out to be the case over twenty years later when my father took us to Oak Forest and made it impossible for my grandma to live in the house she had known as home so many years. Finally, her health failed, and she went to live at Poland's Nursing Home in Sumner. It was an old Victorian house with a wraparound porch and fire escape ladders snaking down along each side. We visited my grandma whenever we came home from Oak Forest. Sometimes, my father convinced her to come out onto the porch, but usually she preferred to sit in her dimly lit room, a blanket over her legs no matter how hot the day. I remember the strong smell of mentholatum from the Deep Heat she rubbed into her muscles, and the sticks of horehound candy she gave me as a treat. "Is that Lee?" she would say, and then she would reach out with her hand, and I would know I was to go to her and let her feel my face.

In those days, I fancied myself a singer. My grandma, when we had all lived on the farm, had taught me hymns: *Jesus Loves Me, Throw Out the Lifeline, Sweet Hour of Prayer*. One day, at the nursing home, she asked me to sing *Blessed Assurance*. She was down in the heart, she said. She felt so low she couldn't even get out of bed. She lay there, the blankets pulled up under her chin, and I watched her cheeks, all hollow and rubbery without her dentures in her mouth, flutter with her breath. "Will you do that for your granny?" she asked. "Just sing her that one song?"

I wanted to, honestly I did. But there were aides coming in and out of the room, and an old man moaning in the hallway, and maybe I felt guilty because we had left my grandma and she had ended up in this sad, sad place. Whatever the reason, I turned shy. I grabbed onto my mother's waist, pressed my face into her side. I heard the voices around me and thought this was what it was like for my grandma who couldn't see.

"Go on," my mother said. She tried to pry me away from her, but I held on tight. "Your grandma wants you to sing."

"Maybe he wants a horehound stick." My grandma's voice was tired and sounded as if it were coming from far away. "Is that what you want, honey?"

I shook my head. Something about the fact that she could be

so concerned about me when obviously she was the one who deserved my consolation, shamed me, and as much as I wanted to sing for her, I couldn't.

"He's being stubborn," my mother finally said, and I knew she was disappointed in me.

"It's all right," said my grandma, and now she sounded embarrassed by my refusal. "Let him be." By this time, I was crying. "Hush now," she said. I felt her fingers brush my arm. "No one's going to make you sing. You just hush."

My betrayal was particularly despicable because she had been the one to save me that night when she had pressed her hot teacup into the bare flesh of my father's arm, and at the one moment when she had asked a simple favor of me I had failed her.

I was thinking about that moment the night she died, ashamed all over again because I hadn't been able to offer her this one kindness. In some small way, I knew what my father was feeling as he drove behind my Uncle Don's Mercury, out past the Texaco refinery with its sprawling towers and bright lights, to my aunt and uncle's bungalow.

In my aunt and uncle's house, my cousin Roger sat quietly on the couch, his hands folded in his lap. He stared at me that night with his sparkling blue eyes, and I felt certain he knew my guilt and would sooner or later announce it. He had that remarkable gift for remembering things about family members. He could recite the birthdays and anniversaries and deaths, and line out the entire family history of who had been born where, who had lived here and there, where they had finally settled and been buried. He was a kind man with the heart of a child who had shown me how to pitch horseshoes, work jigsaw puzzles, do paint-by-numbers. I had no reason to fear him outside the fact that I believed that he was innocent and I was not.

My father's voice was too loud for the small house. "I'll pay for the casket," he said before anyone had even mentioned the funeral expenses.

"We know you can pay for it," my Uncle Don said. "We know you've got the money."

"Seven twenty-three," Roger said. He shifted his penetrating stare to my father. "That's when she died."

Aunt Ruth was smoothing the crocheted doily on the arm of her chair. "So let him pay for it," she said with a sigh. She tipped back her head and closed her eyes. "We'll go to Charlie Sivert's funeral home in the morning and make all the arrangements."

"We'll get the best casket," my father said. "I don't care what it costs."

But when morning came, and we were all gathered at Charlie Sivert's, my Aunt Lucille wouldn't allow it. "We've all been paying for the nursing home," she said. "We'll all pay for the funeral, too."

She had always been the more assertive of my two aunts. She had raised five kids and had a low tolerance for nonsense.

"Beulah," my father said, "write the check."

My mother had the checkbook open on her lap, and I imagined that even her graceful handwriting would be an affront to my aunts. Charlie Sivert got up from behind his desk and told us he would step outside to give us some time to talk things over. He was a soft-spoken man full of patience. "I'll be right outside," he said. "You just let me know when you're ready."

The air in the funeral home smelled of flowers and furniture polish; the carpet was thick and muffled the steps of the living.

My father tapped the point of his hook on the checkbook. "Write it," he told my mother again.

She started to write the date. "February," she wrote, and then she stopped. She raised her head, and there was such a lost look on her face. "I've forgotten the date," she said.

"February 27," said Roger. "1965."

It was Saturday, and ordinarily my parents and I would have been at the junior high gym for my Biddy Basketball League game. We would come home, and at lunch, my father would congratulate me for my good plays and then ask me why I hadn't shot in a certain situation instead of passing the ball or why I hadn't gone all the way to the basket instead of stopping for a jump shot. Who knew, I would want to tell him. At the time, I just did what seemed right to do, as he was now, insisting that my mother write the check that would pay for my grandma's casket.

When it was written, she paused, glanced up at my father. "Are you sure this is what you want to do?" she said.

He looked over at my aunts, and narrowed his eyes. "I'm sure," he said, and like that, it was done.

After the funeral arrangements had been made on Saturday, we drove down to our farm because my father said he wanted to "check on things." We walked into the cold house and went from room to room where our furniture was still in the same arrangement as it had been when my mother and father and grandma and I had lived there. I sat down in my grandma's rocking chair and felt the wooden arms worn smooth by the pressure of her hands, and just like that, before I could stop myself, I was crying. This was the time, had it been an ordinary day, when my father might have spoken sharply to me, irritated by my fussiness, or perhaps even taken off his belt to whip me for being cross. But, to my surprise, he didn't say a word, nor did my mother, and for a while the only noise in the house was the sound of my crying, which seemed to be the lament of all our regrets.

Then my father said, "We should have come as soon as Ruth called." He spoke in an even tone. "We should have told that principal to go to hell."

My mother was straightening the edge of a drape. I remembered that she had stood at that same window two years before, looking out into the dusk, as my father had told my grandma we were moving to Oak Forest. Now my mother turned back to my father, and there were tears in her eyes. "You made the decision to take us there," she said. "You could have made the decision to bring us back."

"I'm not sure anymore," he said, and when he raised his head, I saw regret in his eyes. "I don't know where we belong."

I thought, then, of our apartment in Oak Forest where my father spent his days watching quiz shows on television. I thought of my desk at school which would be empty come Monday, the day of my grandma's funeral, and my mother's classroom where a substitute teacher would take charge. Outside our farmhouse, our collie, Rover, scratched on the door, convinced, as I'm sure he was each time we made a trip to the farm on weekends or holidays, that we had come home to stay.

"We could come back," my mother said. "We could. Isn't this home?"

I imagine now that she must have been thinking about her own mother, who lived alone just two miles to the west of our farm, and how long it would be before a call would come as it had about my Grandma Martin, and there we would be, so far away in a land that would never be completely ours no matter how long we stayed. We had tried to adapt to its people and their manners, but still there were times when we stood out as frauds. Our southern Illinois twangs gave us away, as did our country ways. We would never be as sophisticated as the people we moved among. Once, my father had bought a bottle of champagne and asked my mother to open it for our supper, convinced, I suppose, that this was the custom in the city. The cork exploded from the bottle, smashed into the light globe above our table, and brought slivers of glass falling down into our food. How silly my mother and father must have felt then. How much they must have longed for the place we had left.

"Home is where the heart is," my father said to my mother. "Haven't you ever heard that?"

She said something then that sounded like a teacher's thing to say. It would be years before I would read Frost's "The Death of the Hired Man" in a book of poems she owned and remember her saying it. "Home is the place where, when you have to go there, they have to take you in."

"Yes," my father said, "but first you have to tell them you were wrong. That's their price."

He walked through the house, and my mother and I followed him, not speaking, all of us, I know, cataloging the signs of my grandma having lived there: the scratches on the stovepipe in the kitchen where she had scraped a match each morning to light a gas ring on the range, the jar of Sanka coffee still on the counter, her sunbonnet hanging from a nail beside the back door, the scents of Tums antacids and Black Draught laxative powder and horehound candy that came wafting up from a nightstand drawer when my mother opened it.

My father sat down on the bed. "I wish we could stay here," he said, "instead of going to Lucille's."

We had spent the last two nights at Aunt Lucille's instead of going to the farmhouse where it would have taken at least a day to light the fuel oil stoves and let them take out the cold. I could see my father's breath, and I thought of the snow we had driven through only to be in this place where I was shivering, this house we had once called home. We had no choice but to leave it, to go back to my aunt's.

"Well," she said when we walked into her house. "Was everything the way it was when you left it?"

"Everything was fine," my father said.

Then we ate the food Aunt Lucille cooked for us, and we slept in the beds she had made up with fresh sheets, and the next day, Sunday afternoon, we went to the funeral home for my grandma's wake. I saw her lying in the casket my father had paid for, and she looked much as she had the day in the nursing home when she had asked me to sing *Blessed Assurance*, and I had denied her, only now the hollows of her cheeks weren't moving with the rise and fall of her breath, and her eyes were closed, and there was a blue tinge, just barely visible, to her skin.

I remembered the times I had lain in bed with her when we had lived on the farm, and she had told me stories about how my great-grandfather, James Henry Martin, had built the farmhouse and how she and my grandfather had moved there to take care of James Henry after my great-grandmother, Mary Ann, had died. "That was the way it was done," she had explained to me. "The kids always looked after the old ones."

She had expected a similar favor from my father, but he had left her. She had asked me to sing for her, and I had refused.

The morning of the funeral, I wouldn't get out of bed. I woke with the thought of my grandma's casket being buried in the ground. I had been with my parents to the cemeteries on Decoration Day, and I had seen the graves of my grandfather and my great-grandfather and my grandma's two babies who had died. I understood what it was to be a living person one day, and then to be put into the ground, and the thought, now that this was true about someone I had actually known and with whom I had moved through the world, terrified me, and I couldn't bear the thought of watching my grandma's casket buried.

"I'm not going," I told my mother.

The sun was streaming through the window, and my mother

was sitting on the edge of the bed, patting my back. "Oh, you have to go," she said. "It's your last chance to see your grandma."

I pressed my face into my pillow. My mother tried to lift me from the bed, but I squirmed and kicked, and squalled. I could smell coffee brewing and eggs cooking; I could hear bacon sizzling in Aunt Lucille's frying pan.

"Aren't you hungry?" my mother said.

"No," I told her.

"Oh, I bet you are. I bet you'd like some bacon." No matter how much she wheedled and enticed, I wouldn't budge. "All right," she finally said. "I guess you want to be stubborn. Today of all days." Then she got up from the bed and left the room.

I didn't mean to be a problem, but unfortunately I was, an annoyance my parents could have done without. I thought of them in the kitchen with Aunt Lucille and Uncle Mick. I thought of Aunt Ruth and Uncle Don and Roger in their rented bungalow, everyone making ready for my grandma's funeral, everyone up and ready to face the day, everyone but me. I recalled the night my grandma had saved me from my father's whipping. Her voice had been firm. "You leave that boy alone." Now I couldn't even get out of bed to go to her funeral. It wasn't that I didn't want to, but now that I had resisted, I had put myself into a position beyond which innocence was impossible. Even if I were to walk out into the kitchen, penitent, I would be, in the eyes of everyone waiting there, guilty of being difficult on a day when misery was the property of the adults.

The bedroom door opened, and I heard footsteps on the floor. I smelled cigarette smoke, and I knew it was my Uncle Mick sitting on the bed. "Honey," he said. "Do you have a stomachache? Is that what's bothering you?"

Usually, he liked to pester me by giving me Dutch rubs that left my hair sticking out in wild tufts and my scalp on fire. His kindness now shamed me even more, and I buried my head further under my pillow and waited for him to leave me alone.

"Honey, you don't want to be this way," he said, and then he was gone.

Now I was like the man on the ledge of a tall tall building, a man who had meant to jump, but then all these people had come and begged him not to, and even though he wanted to come back inside and go on with living, he knew he would always be the crazy guy who had said he would jump and how would he ever live that down.

The next time the door opened, I heard my father say to my mother, "Just leave us alone for a while. I'll take care of this."

I knew what this usually meant, a whipping to make me behave. I heard my father tap his hooks together, the way he did whenever he wanted to turn one of them to the right angle so he could pick something up with it. I waited to hear the sound I knew so well, the jangle of his belt buckle, the slap of leather as he yanked the belt from his trousers, the whistle the belt made slashing through the air just before it fell across my skin.

But all I heard was my father pushing the door closed. Then he came across the room, and he lay down next to me on the bed, and for a good while he didn't speak. Then finally he said, "It's an unusual day, isn't it?" I thought of how, at that moment, I should have been in Mrs. Malley's class saying the Pledge of Allegiance. "Such a strange day." He sighed. "You'd hardly think it was meant for you."

I could hear the radio playing softly in the kitchen. Outside, my Uncle Mick's oil pumps were squealing, and a tardy rooster was crowing. So much in the world seemed normal, but inside me, and I know now this was true for my father as well, something felt odd, because my grandma was gone, and we both felt guilty over how we had treated her.

"Hear that?" my father said. "Mr. Rooster's all mixed up. He must have slept through the dawn. He must have been an old lazy bones. Now he's too late."

I heard my father's voice break, and it startled me. I pulled my head out from under my pillow and saw him lying on his back, his eyes closed, his hooks clasped on top of his stomach. "When I die," he had said, as we had left my grandma's wake, "everyone will come just to see if they bury me with these hooks." It was, perhaps, the first time I understood that my father, so much older than my friends' fathers, might die while I was young. And though he was the man who whipped me, he was my father, and freedom from him would carry with it an everlasting guilt, a regret that we hadn't found a way to love each other more.

It was impossible for me to snuggle in close to him, because of his hooks, but I moved as close as I could and felt the heat from his body.

"We have to go," he said. "You know that, don't you?"

I didn't answer. In a while, he would ask me if I was ready, and we would rise and go to the funeral home. But for the moment, we lay there, the two of us alone, while the rooster crowed again and my father said, "Good morning," as if we were just then waking to a new day.

SIX

In the summers, we came back to the farm and stayed until school started again in September. One summer, the school board in Oak Forest insisted that my mother finish her degree. This was in 1967, and she was fifty-seven years old. That summer, she lived in a rooming house in Charleston and came home on the weekends, an arrangement I despised because I hated being alone with my father.

"Hold it still," he told me one morning. We were in the barn, setting steel traps for the raccoons and groundhogs that came to feed on our corn and beans. "Easy now. We're almost home."

The trap rested on a piece of planking so he could step down on the prongs of the spring-tension handle and spread the trap's jaws. It was my job to reach my fingers down into the middle of those jaws and lift a round paddle, the size of a quarter, and slide it into the slot at the end of a steel tab. I had to hold it there while my father stepped off the handle. If I let go too soon, the paddle slipped away from the tab, and we had to start again. Sometimes the timing was such that my father eased off the handles, and the trap's jaws snapped shut, the breeze flicking across my barely escaping fingers. "You didn't hold it," he said then, his voice harsh with reproach. "I told you to hold it still."

I wanted to please him, particularly that summer when my mother was away all week at the university and he depended on me, but I could tell, even then, that I wasn't the sort of boy he would have chosen as his son.

After we set the traps, we slid them under the mangers where the raccoons and groundhogs had dug away the dirt. There were chains at the ends of the traps and we wired them to the manger slats. "All right now," my father said. "Let's see what we can catch."

It was my job, every morning, to crouch by the mangers and pull each trap out by its chain. I can still remember the moment just before I pulled when I didn't know whether I would feel a weight at the other end. I prayed that I wouldn't, because when I did, I had to pull the raccoon or groundhog out into the open where my father bludgeoned it to death with his hook. I remember the way the animals hissed and screamed, the way they tried to squirm back under the manger, an escape I closed off by tugging hard on the chain. "Hold him," my father shouted. "Hold him." He brought his hook down again and again as I felt the raccoon or groundhog straining away from me, desperately trying to get free from what held it.

So often that summer, my father asked me to do something beyond my limits: to loosen a rusted nut on a piece of machinery, to lift a cultivator and pin it with cotter keys to the tractor, to set the steel traps. "I can't," I often told him, and he replied, "Can't never did nothing. Try it again."

I imagine he had forgotten what it felt like to pinch a finger, scrape a knuckle, smash a thumb. The tempered steel of his hooks had been crafted to withstand heat and pressure. When we washed dishes, he plunged those hooks into water so hot I couldn't bear it. We had no running water in our farmhouse, so we filled a dish pan and set it to boil on the stove. "Get it hot," he always said. "I can take it."

He said this with pride, and it was clear that he enjoyed putting his hooks into the scalding water if for no other reason than to remind me that he was rugged—"The hotter the better," he said—and that if I dared disobey him, it would be no skin off his nose to make me pay the price.

One day, I was trying to loosen a stubborn nut on a harrow tooth. The crescent wrench kept slipping, and each time it did, my hand scraped across the harrow frame and sent a fire across my skin.

"You don't have it set right," my father said. He was on his knees beside me. "Tighten it up."

It was hot, even there in the shade of our maple tree, and I was tired of banging up my hand, tired of the gnats flying around my face. I knew, one way or another, the nut had to come off, but because the farm wasn't my responsibility, I was ready to give up much sooner than my father. I wanted to go into the house and get a Pepsi-Cola from the refrigerator, and turn on the television. I wanted to lie on the cool linoleum, the oscillating fan stirring the air over me, and forget about the harrow and the nut that refused to turn. The truth was I wanted to be far, far away from my father.

But there was no way he would let me escape. He had to replace that harrow tooth, and the only way to do that was to loosen that nut. Because my mother was sixty miles away in Charleston, I was the one who had to do it. I could recall all the times she had been the one to wield wrenches for my father, and how, sometimes, when she would have a difficult time with a piece of machinery, he would speak sharply to her, frustrated, I suspect, not only by her inadequacy, but also because he wished he could do the job. I thought of her in her rooming house in Charleston. I imagined her sitting at her desk, the window open, a breeze lifting the curtains and then letting them fall back as she turned another page of a book, stopped to jot something down in her notebook, her fountain pen gliding across the smooth, white paper. I saw how simple her life was there compared to the life she had with my father and me, and I began to fear that she would never come back to us.

That's when I started to cry.

"What are you bawling about?" my father said.

"My hand," I told him.

"That's just a scratch. You're all right."

I dropped the crescent wrench to the ground. "It hurts," I said.

"A little scratch, and you're bawling like a baby. Wah, wah, wah. You want me to make you a sugar tit?"

I knew he was trying to shame me into picking up the crescent wrench and getting back to my chore, and because I knew that, I stubbornly refused to do it. I was too young and willful to appreciate that he was trying to teach me perseverance. I was as intractable as the nut on the harrow tooth and so was he.

"Go to hell," I said. His offer of a sugar tit, which he often made when he was trying to humiliate me, hurt my feelings and left me raw with indignation. I scrambled to my feet. "You can do it yourself."

I started to the house. Behind me, my father called out, "You come back here." I kept walking. I heard the slap of leather as his hook pulled out the tongue of his belt. "Mister, I'm warning you," he said.

He caught up to me just as I was about to open the back door. His belt came down across the small of my back, and I jumped away from the sting. I landed in my mother's flower bed, breaking down a marigold, which seemed to enrage my father more. The belt came down again, this time on the back of my thigh.

I turned and grabbed the belt, catching the lash in my palm. I held the belt a moment and felt my father tug on it. I pulled back, and it came free from his grasp.

For just an instant, he glanced down at his hook as if he couldn't believe the belt was gone. Then he looked at me, his eyes narrowed, the worry line in his forehead deepening with his rage. He took a step toward me. That's when I threw the belt out into the grass, and turned and ran.

I ran down our lane, the hot air rushing up into my face. My father chased after me. I heard the furious huffing of his breath, his boots kicking through the gravel. I imagined, at any moment, his hook would reach out and snare me. But he was fifty-four years old that summer, and I quickly outdistanced him. I ran and ran, stopping finally at the end of our lane. I turned back to our house and saw him atop the small hill just beyond our hickory tree. His cap had flown off his head, and he was kneeling in the gravel, trying to pick it up with his hook. I was sobbing, choking for breath, scared to death now because I knew I had no choice but to go back.

When I finally did, my father was sitting on the grass by the harrow, trying to fit the crescent wrench to the nut. "I can't adjust it," he said, and his voice was meek.

I sat down on the grass beside him. "Do you want it smaller or bigger?"

"Smaller," he told me, and he let the wrench drop from his hook. I picked it up, rubbed my thumb over the calibration wheel and tried to close the jaws just a fraction. "That's it," he said, encouraging me with a patience that made me sorry for the anger between us. "We'll just keep trying, won't we? Until we get it right."

On Friday afternoons, my father and I either drove to Charleston to get my mother or to Olney where we waited in the city park until she appeared, having caught a ride with another woman. These were the sweetest days. Even my father was in high spirits. He came in from the field at noon, and after we had eaten lunch-meat sandwiches and cleaned the kitchen, we set about making ready to present ourselves to my mother. To this day, I am firmly convinced that the one thing my father and I always shared through our difficulties was our profound love and respect for her.

That summer, I did for him what she would do for twenty-six years without regret or complaint; I shaved him, I bathed him, I cleaned him after he had used the toilet. I was eleven years old, and I knew my father's body as intimately as I knew my own: the gray whiskers that grew on his face; the wrinkled craw of his throat, red from the sun; the white flesh, loose on his chest; the swell of his belly; the tuft of pubic hair; the uncircumcised penis; the loins and scrotal sac often inflamed with heat rash. "I'm gall*d*ed," he would say, adding a "d" to the past tense of "gall." I rubbed him tenderly with a wash cloth, patted him dry with a towel, and then powdered him with cornstarch.

Never was he as timid as he was then—as bashful as I. He would look away from me while I washed him, sorry that circumstances were such that I had to perform this task. If anyone were to have seen us there, the aging man and his son, they would have never suspected the ugly rancor that simmered between us. They would have seen the boy soaking the washcloth in a basin of water and wringing it out with his small hands, and the father, standing naked in the sunlight streaming in through the window, his legs apart so his son could touch the washcloth gently to his tender groin. How could I not love him, then, so great was his need. "Burns like fire," he often muttered under his breath. At those times, I concentrated on maintaining a gentle touch, one that wouldn't hurt him. As my mother had done, I rolled fresh white cotton arm socks over his stumps and safety-pinned them to his T-shirt sleeves. I helped him slip his arms into the holsters of his hooks and then settle the canvas straps of the harness across his back.

We stood before the wardrobe, and he chose a shirt and a pair of trousers. He made his choices carefully, matching colors and styles. "Blue," he might say. "Your mother likes blue." When he was finally satisfied, I dressed him. I buttoned his shirt, held his trousers so he could step into them. I fastened his belt. The finishing touch was a dab of Butch Hair Creme brushed through his flat top. He would turn his head this way and that, looking at himself in the dresser mirror.

"Ready?" he would finally say, and I would race to the door, my heart light and full of joy because my mother was coming home.

She brought her laundry and her schoolbooks. Saturday mornings, I woke to the chirr of the wringer washing machine on the back porch, and I lay in bed, content to let the cool morning breeze drift over me, to listen to birds singing outside my window. My father would drive to the Berryville Store and come back with glazed doughnuts. My mother steeped hot tea, and we sat at the kitchen table, I still in my pajamas, and enjoyed the doughnuts and the tea and talked about what had taken place in the week my mother had been gone. My father bragged about his crops: the wheat, golden and nearly ready to cut; the soybeans, lush and green; the corn, as high as his waist. He told my mother what he cooked for the two of us, how we washed the dishes. He never spoke of the times we got angry with each other, nor did I. Neither of us wanted to ruin the calm of those Saturday mornings when my mother was back in our house.

My father spent those days in the fields, and if everything ran smoothly, he never called for my mother's help. Then, she was mine. I was so crazy to have her, I did the chores she assigned me without a peep of protest. I helped her hang the clothes outside to dry. I dusted and swept. I chatted with her while she did the ironing. I leafed through her textbooks, particularly fascinated by her

entomology book with its diagrams of butterflies and grasshop-
pers and moths. She was collecting insects for her class, and late in
the afternoon, when the housework was finally done, we went out
into the tall thickets of grass around our barn lot with her butter-
fly net.

One day, we saw a monarch feeding on a milkweed pod.
"That's a prize," my mother said, and then she explained to me
how the monarchs had just begun to appear there on the Illinois
prairie, returning from Mexico where they had migrated for the
winter.

"Mexico?" I knew where it was from my geography class. "How
do they get all the way down there?"

"They fly. Can you imagine? All that way. Such delicate wings."

The monarch's wings were orangish brown and laced with black
veins. They pulsed, rising and falling a bit. "How do they know
the way?" I imagined all the miles and miles to Mexico, the wide
expanse of sky.

"They just know. Even though they've never been there. Isn't
that something? It's a miracle of nature, I guess."

I had been her miracle, surviving the increased odds that I
would be a Down's syndrome baby because of her age.

The pulsing of the monarch's wings was as regular as breath.
"It's pretty," I said.

My mother nodded. "In Mexico, people say the monarchs are
the souls of dead children lifting up to heaven." She bit down on
her lip. "Listen to me. What a thing to say. Do you hate your
mother for saying that?"

I remembered the day my Grandma Martin had told me about
my father's brother and sister, Owen and Lola, who had died in
their second summers. I shook my head. "It's nice to go to heaven,
isn't it?"

"Yes, it's nice," my mother told me, but I could tell, from her sad smile, that she would be a long time forgiving herself for her comment, one that had reminded both of us that sometimes children died.

Perhaps it grieved her because she had lost her childhood early in life as soon as she was old enough to help care for her brothers and sisters. She had become a woman of duty and endurance, selfless and without need, at least none she was willing to place before the obligation she felt toward her family. The eight of them—my grandfather and grandmother, and the six children—lived for a while on a farm south of Berryville, but my grandfather couldn't keep up with the mortgage payments, and the bank foreclosed. His name was Harrison Read, and I never knew him since he died shortly after I was born. In the photographs I have of him, he seems like a gentle man, tall and thin, but with a sad face and sloped shoulders as if the burden of his life, and the poor choices he made in it, eventually wore him down. The way I understand it, from stories various relatives have told, he had a drinking problem. More than once, he ended up in the Olney jail, arrested for public drunkenness, and my Uncle Homer had to bail him out. Fortunately, for all involved, my grandfather was a sad drunk instead of a mean one, and, if he could have only given up liquor, which he eventually managed to do, he would have lived a pleasant life, enjoying the Zane Grey novels he read aloud to his children each evening, the pet raccoon he fed from a baby bottle, the St. Louis Cardinals' baseball games he listened to on the radio. I would gather these facts about him much later, when, as an adult, I would start to ask my aunts and uncles for stories. When I was a child, not old enough for school, I spent the days with my Grandma Read. There was a library table in her bedroom, and she forbade me from opening its drawer, an order I, of course, disobeyed. Inside the drawer were two cigarette lighters, a packet of pipe cleaners, a tin of Prince Albert tobacco, a deck of Bicycle playing cards. These were my grandfather's last possessions, and my grandmother, though she couldn't bring herself to throw them out, feared that if I handled them I would soak up whatever darkness had tainted him and brought him to drink.

My mother had tried to save him. One day, she found all the whiskey bottles he had hid in the shed and set them on the front steps, hoping to shame him into quitting his drinking, but as far as I know, her ploy didn't work. He lost the farm, and for a while, he and my grandmother moved to the northern part of the state and worked at the state hospital in Dixon. When they came back, he leased the Berryville General Store. My mother, after she had dismissed her pupils for the day, worked in the store. I can imagine her slicing luncheon meat, weighing fruit on the scale, testing the cream the farmers brought to sell, her attention on making the proper measurement, the exact change, believing that she was holding the world in balance, ensuring that my grandfather, who had stopped drinking, had even become a member of the church, would continue to live the decent, orderly life she had always wished for him. As a young girl, she had taken care of her brothers and sisters; now she was safeguarding her father and mother. She lived in their house, worked in their store, convinced, I suspect, that her presence was necessary to their continued good fortune. Surely she dreamed no life for herself, no husband or child, until she met my father and was so overwhelmed with loneliness she mustered her courage and decided to start a life with him.

He must have been as lonely as she for he lived on the farm, two miles east of Berryville, caring for his mother. His sisters had married and left home and started families. He was the one who stayed. I can imagine him coming in from his chores to cook for my grandmother, to help her measure out her medicines. I picture his hands wielding a paring knife as he peels potatoes or delicately balances a medicine dropper above my grandmother's cloudy eyes.

I see him, after she has gone to bed, listening to a Cardinals' game on the radio, the volume turned low so as not to wake her. He doodles on a Farm Bureau pamphlet, writes his name over and over, the way someone might practice the name of his beloved. Or if it's Saturday night, he puts on a clean shirt, tries to press his best trousers, combs his hair with Wildroot tonic, and leaves for the Berryville Store where he will help my mother carry milk cans into the storage locker, willing to put up with the kidding he'll get later about making sure he's old enough to woo a woman, all for her company. He knows the way as well as he knows anything—the mile to the crossroads and the mile west to the store. He likes to see his truck's headlights stretching their beams out into the darkness, catching the glint of wire fences, whitewashing the gravel roadbed, illuminating, finally, the metal Pepsi-Cola sign atop the storefront. Sometimes he leaves the lights on a moment after he has parked in front of the store, lets them shine through the window, until my mother, at the cash register, turns, shades her eyes. Then he switches off the lights so she can see he has finally come.

On Saturday nights, when my mother was home from the university, we drove into Sumner where we bought groceries, and my father loafed at the pool hall or the barber shop, and my mother went to Harry Bartram's Beauty Salon where she had her hair done. I went with her and sat in the swing on the front porch and read comic books until the light faded. Then I listened to the Cardinals' game on the radio Mr. Bartram kept playing inside. I waited until my mother was finished, and then we walked uptown to find my father.

One night, he came for us. I was sitting inside the beauty shop when I heard his footsteps on the porch, saw his shadowy form fill the doorway. He opened the screen door and stepped inside. "I've come to get you," he said to my mother. "You and Lee."

She was slipping some money from her billfold to pay Mr. Bartram. "Oh, we could have walked," she said. I imagine that she secretly enjoyed the minutes we spent strolling alone together beneath the canopy of the oak trees that lined the street.

"Not tonight," he said, and his voice was tight with worry. "There might be trouble tonight."

"Trouble?" My mother patted her fresh hairdo. "What kind of trouble?"

"Boyd Brian's uptown with a butcher knife. He's on a tear."

"Drunk again, I imagine," Mr. Bartram said.

"Drunk as a lord," said my father.

The story was this. Boyd Brian, drunk, had taken exception to two teenage boys who had stopped to talk to some girls on the porch of a house across from the barber shop. "Don't ask me why," my father said when we were in our car. I sat in the backseat and listened to him tell this story in a low voice. He told how Boyd Brian had fetched a butcher knife from his house and had used it to threaten the boys. Then he had gone up and down Main Street, ranting and raving. "I wouldn't want you and Lee to meet up with him," my father said. "He's a damned lunatic tonight."

I had never known my father as someone who would want to protect me, and it was difficult to reconcile that image of him with the one I knew best.

"I want to go home," I said from the backseat. We had turned down Main Street and were headed uptown to do our grocery shopping. We passed the dark windows of *The Sumner Press* office, the marquee of the Idaho Theater, the television store where a set in the window was playing. Normally, there would have been people parked in front, sitting on the hoods of their cars to watch whatever program was on. The fact that they weren't made the town seem dangerous to me, made whatever harmony my mother brought to us on the weekends seem precarious. I thought of the raccoons and groundhogs burrowing beneath our mangers, feeling their way through the darkness, not knowing that the traps were there, the steel jaws waiting to spring shut at the first wrong step. "I want to go home," I said again, but my father was parking the car in front of Ferguson's Grocery, and my mother was opening her pocketbook to find her shopping list.

"I'll just be a minute." She turned around and looked at me. "Lee, are you coming with me, or are you staying here?"

My father answered for me. "He's staying here. If he goes, it'll take you longer."

She opened the door, and, at that moment, we heard a blast. Its echo went on and on. People came out from the stores and stood on the sidewalk. I saw a man lift his arm and point behind us, down the narrow side street, lined with two-story frame houses. I rose up on my knees and looked out the back glass of our car. I could see the light from the street lamps splintering through the trees, the shadows of the houses, porch lights coming on. I heard dogs barking, a screen door slap shut.

My mother turned and looked at my father. She had the car door open. She had one foot on the pavement outside. "Go inside the store," he told her. "Take Lee and go inside." I knew, then, that what we had heard had been a gunshot.

Men were running now past our car, running down the narrow street toward the echo of the shot. "Go ahead," my father said, and my mother got out of the car. She opened the back door and reached for me. I took her hand and let her lead me quickly into Ferguson's Grocery. The clerks were standing at the windows, their long white aprons tied around their waists. My mother and I turned to look out the window, and I saw my father getting out of the car. He started walking down the side street along with other men, following those who had run.

My mother grabbed a wire shopping basket and started down the aisle. "Let's see," she said, studying her shopping list, "what do we need for you and your father?"

We were the only shoppers, and it felt strange to make our way up and down the aisles, alone, as if we had accidentally been locked in the store overnight. Then customers started coming back into the store, and I heard fragments of conversation: "Boyd Brian," "his boy, Jack Brian," "a twelve-gauge," "both barrels."

It wasn't until later, when my father stopped at my Uncle Mick's farm, that I understood exactly what had happened. My mother and I stayed in the car while my father went to my uncle's door. I could hear them talking softly in the night.

"Boyd Brian's boy shot him," my father said.

"Kill him?" asked my Uncle Mick.

"Point-blank," my father told him. "Shot his head off."

I could hear the oil pumps squealing in my uncle's fields, could see the bright flames of the gas flares.

"I suspect Boyd asked for it." Uncle Mick leaned forward and spit a stream of tobacco juice out into the yard. "He was a mean sonofabitch. Treated those kids awful. Someone should have killed him years ago. How old is that boy?"

"Old enough to fire both barrels of a twelve-gauge. I expect they'll lock him away for it."

"What you think about that?" my Uncle Mick asked.

My father glanced back at our car, then, and I imagined he was looking for me there in the dark. What was he thinking? That there was too much life ahead of us, too much that could go wrong? Or was he only checking to see whether I was listening? He turned back to my uncle, leaned in close. "They ought to give him a medal," he said in a fierce whisper, and in that moment, something went out into the air and closed itself around my father and me. I imagined Boyd Brian's son, a boy I didn't know, and he became real to me. I knew his terror, his rage. My father knew it, too. "A goddamn medal," he said again, this time in a hiss as slow and as difficult as a last breath, words he didn't mean for me to hear.

SEVEN

The summer Boyd Brian's son shot and killed him was the only summer I spent alone with my father. In August, my mother went through graduation ceremonies and received her degree. We went back to Oak Forest, and two years later, in the spring of 1969, I graduated from the eighth grade.

That spring, my father often picked me up after school and then drove to Kimberly Heights Elementary where we waited for my mother to finish marking a set of papers or to prepare her lesson plans. Sometimes he let me slide over next to him and take the wheel and steer while he operated the gas pedal and the brake. "We're sailing now," he often said to me. "That's the ticket. Now we're a team."

At Kimberly Heights he usually went in to shoot the breeze with the custodian or to wait in my mother's room. I stayed in the car, turning on the ignition key so I could listen to WLS on the radio. As I sang along with The Association, Three Dog Night, Donovan, I kept my eye on the side view mirror so I could see my parents when they came out of the school. Then I turned off the ignition before they knew what I was up to. My father, had he known, would have yelled at me for running down the car battery, and the high spirits of the day would have slipped away from us.

"Ready, Mr. Navigator?" my father always asked when he and my mother were in the car.

"Roger," I told him.

And off we would go to find houses for sale, addresses that my father had earlier marked on the city map. After six years in Oak Forest, my parents had decided to stay so I would have better opportunities in high school than I would in the small school I would attend if we were to go back to our farm. I held the city map spread open on my lap and traced the lines my father had drawn with a pencil. I imagined him in our apartment, picking up the pencil with his hook and drawing those crooked lines. I imagined him trying to maneuver the pencil across the map, those shaky lines so full of purpose and hope, and a tremendous feeling of love ambushed me, rose up, despite all the years of difficulty between us.

"You just tell me where to turn," he said.

And I called out the streets, the intersections and the dead ends, while my mother sat in the backseat, murmuring from time to time. "Mercy," she said. "Would you look at that? Isn't it grand?"

We drove into the new subdivisions that had gone up all around the edges of Oak Forest and looked at houses. We drove down streets with pretty names—Debra Drive, Tiffany Trail, Lilac Lane. My father pulled our car to the curb, and we sat staring out at brick homes on freshly-sodded lots.

"You want a good foundation," he usually said. "A good foundation and a solid roof. That's the important stuff."

For six years, we had lived in our rented duplex that we sublet in the summers so we could go back to our farm. I grew up caught between two cultures, the rural and the urban, never quite sure where I belonged. In southern Illinois, my old friends called me "city slicker"; when I came back to Oak Forest in the fall, my friends there called me "hillbilly." I suppose, given the choice, I preferred the city since I had become, in the six years I had spent there, an earnest boy, in love with books and music and pursuits of the mind. The people on the farms of southern Illinois valued the body. Boys went barefoot and shirtless in the summers and turned brown in the sun. They drove tractors and worked the hay-fields, and when they weren't sweating over their chores, they fished and hunted or went skinny-dipping in ponds. I never felt completely at home with them since I was more reserved, more timid, and though I could match them with athletic skill, I shied away from their contests of strength and daring—their wrestling matches; their games of "Flinch," where they punched each other as hard as they could in the arms; their mock battles where they used air rifles to pepper each other with BB's. I preferred, instead, the graceful dance required on a basketball court, or the acrobatic dives and leaps it sometimes took to catch a baseball on the diamond.

The days we drove into the subdivisions and walked through the homes for sale, my mother meekly opened kitchen cabinets and looked inside. My father paced off the backyards, planning, I imagine, where he might put in a garden plot, where he might plant shrubs and trees. I looked out the windows and saw the neighborhood boys riding their stingray bicycles down the streets, lingering in front of lawns where girls sat listening to transistor radios. Sometimes a mother came out on the steps and called for a son or a daughter in a lilting voice. Often, as we left a subdivison, dusk would be falling and lights would be coming on in the houses. I would see the bright paintings on the walls, the pianos, the spiral staircases winding between levels, the families sitting down to their dinners. Sometimes they would bow their heads, and I would imagine the father's low voice asking the blessing. I would wonder what it would be like if that were my family, my home, and I was going there. Then we would be past them, our car gathering speed, my father driving on into the coming dark.

*   *   *

One of my friends that year was a boy named Larry Albiero. He lived with his sister and his parents in a split-level house in a subdivision very much like the ones my father took us to on those spring evenings. Larry's life was everything mine wasn't. His father was a distinguished man with hair graying at the temples and a tan year-round from sunlamps at his health club. He wore suits and ties, even to our basketball games, where he sat in the bleachers, his back straight with his perfect posture, one leg crossed neatly over the other. He worked for the S & H Green Stamp Company. My parents collected those trading stamps from grocery stores and filling stations and pasted them into paper booklets. Once or twice a year, they took them to a redemption center and exchanged them for small household items, perhaps a wastebasket, or a napkin holder, or a soap dish. Mr. Albiero, because he was a trading stamp bigshot, brought home a billiard table, an English touring bike for Larry, a color television. They had a hi-fi stereo, a water cooler, a barbecue grill, a jukebox, a piano, a collection of Oriental vases.

"We're a redemption house," Mr. Albiero liked to say, and I know that when I was there, I felt I'd found a place of refuge.

Larry's sister, Paulette, was a musician. Often, in the evening, when I was there, we would all gather to listen to her play the piano. I liked the way she tossed her long, black hair over her shoulders as she settled herself on the piano bench. When she played, I closed my eyes and felt the notes stirring the air. I breathed them in and let them vibrate in my chest. When she had finished a piece, there was always a bittersweet moment when the last note lingered in the air and no one spoke, and there was only that sound fading to nothing. Then Mrs. Albiero would say, "Bravo," in her delightful southern drawl, and clap her small hands together. "Well done," Mr. Albiero would say, and Larry would roll his eyes at me, not knowing how much I loved being in his house where music filled the air instead of curses and shouts.

Sometimes I came home late, past the hour when my parents had expected me, and my father gave me the third degree. Who did I think I was, he wanted to know. Did I think I could come and go as I pleased? There were rules. Eight o'clock meant eight o'clock. Keep it up, mister, and you'll get yourself in Dutch. He would pick and carp at me until finally I would snap. "Shut up," I would say, or worse, "Go to hell." Our voices would rise and swirl though our duplex, and my mother would plead with us to be quiet. "He can't talk to me like that," my father would say. "I'll give you something to moan about. You're grounded, mister. Two weeks. You don't go anywhere and none of your buddies come here. Now how do you like them apples, *kemosabe?*"

I didn't. I didn't like them at all, but it was easier to fight with my father than to tell him the truth: I was finding other people in the world, families that lived more settled, civil lives, and I wanted to stay with them as long as I could. Sometimes I even dreamed that I lived in a house like the Albieros', and in the evening my mother played the piano, and my father sat in his easy chair reading his newspaper. In these dreams, he always had hands, and he called me "sport," and we went out onto our green lawn and tossed a baseball back and forth as dusk fell, and our voices echoed softly in the still air. "Atta boy," he said to me. "That's the ticket, sport. That's bringing the heat. Yes, sir. You're really pumping the gas."

In the real life I lived, my father could sometimes be charming, and there were small pleasures we often enjoyed. We liked to watch basketball games together on television—the balletic choreography of leaps and spins. Together, we worshipped the hook shot, grew humble in the presence of the behind-the-back dribble, respected the feathery touch of a pure shooter. Sometimes he took me to the high school where we sat on the bleachers and watched boys who, only a few years before, had played at my junior high. "You'll be better than any of them," he said once. "You're a dead-eye. You can really tickle those nets." I've read since that the sports we adore are the ones in which the sounds of completion aesthetically please us—the crack of the bat against the baseball, the smack of a glove against a boxer's face, the pock of a tennis racket's solid strike. For my father and me, it was the swish of a basketball though the net when the shot was dead center, the gentle whisk of leather through cotton, the spin of the ball just right, the arc and drop perfect, more perfect than we could ever hope to be.

His only complaint with my playing was that sometimes I was too timid on the court, too hesitant to get in under the boards and fight for rebounds. "Don't be a sissy," he told me from time to time. "Get in there and show them what's what."

It was true that I often backed away from physical contact, not because I feared it, but because in some way it reminded me of the violence between my father and me. If my private life was going to be filled with open hostility, I had determined that my public life would be reserved and gentle.

One night that spring, my parents took me to the high school to register for my freshman year. It was a large school, and we had to find the right door and then walk past other kids and their parents to the room where we would meet with a counselor. I saw several kids I knew from my junior high. Their parents were much younger than mine. The mothers wore their hair in stunning sweeps and stacks. My mother's hair was gray and cut short so she could more easily manage her natural wave. Already, at fifty-nine, she had started to walk with the stoop in her back that would continue to tip her forward as she aged. She wore rubber-soled oxfords that squeaked on the tile floor instead of clicking smartly like the high-heeled pumps the other mothers wore. The fathers were jaunty in sport coats or cardigan sweaters. They shook hands and patted one another on the back. My father wore a hat, though spring had come and men now went bareheaded. It was a tweed fedora, one of many he had bought since we had moved to Oak Forest, each of them with a small red feather stuck into the band. He left on the hat, even after we had come into the school. He kept his hooks clasped close to his stomach, as if he were trying to make them less noticeable, which, of course, was impossible.

I had never gotten used to the attention those hooks drew, the furtive glances from people trying not to be rude, the out-and-out stares from others who were so surprised to see the prostheses that they couldn't begin to mask their curiosity. Sometimes babies, fascinated, I suppose, by the silver glint of the steel, reached out to touch the hooks. Their own hands were so dainty and pink, the small fingers just beginning to latch onto things. What must it have done to my father to see the delicate flesh on the cold steel? Did it remind him of the photograph I would eventually inherit from him, the one of him as a baby, his dimpled hands holding onto a fluff of feathers? Whenever a baby laid its hand on his hook, he looked off into the distance as if the child's touch were a loving gesture he didn't deserve. I could see how uncomfortable he was, as was I, each for the same reason, I assume: the child's caress made us both ashamed of the unforgiving spirit that persisted between us.

And it was our secret: mine and my father's and my mother's. We carried it with us as we moved through the world, hid it from those who knew us only as the quiet boy, graceful and stoic on the basketball court; the chatty man with no hands, who was always quick to do a good turn for someone who needed his help; the soft-spoken schoolteacher who was like a grandmother to her students. To those who saw us, the only oddities they must have noticed were my parents' age and my father's hooks, each of which was enough to embarrass me.

At the high school that night was a girl named Rita Burns. Back in the winter, her mother had tried to kill herself by taking a bottle of aspirin after her husband had left her, but Rita had found her and called for an ambulance, and Mrs. Burns hadn't died. She was a PTA officer, a band mother, and, of course, everyone was shocked when they found out what she had done. Rita was a pretty girl with dark hair and delicate features. She played the flute in the school band, and she had a nice smile, and was the sort of girl everyone liked. Unlike the stunning girls who were cheerleaders, and more than a little arrogant, she was without affectation. Still, after the episode with her mother, people began to shy away from her as if she were somehow tainted. One night, around this time, I had to go to Larry Albiero's house because his sister was the accompanist for some of the band members who were competing in that year's district solo contest. Rita Burns was there, and it was such an odd feeling to be near her now that her family's life had opened to the world and shown itself to be less than perfect. I remember how her narrow hands, the tendons and veins standing out along their backs, trembled as she played her flute. The tones seemed hollow with grief, the way wind does when it rises and falls in the night and moans its sad song. Listening to her play, surely none of us could help but think of how difficult it was for her to stand there before us, knowing that we were all thinking of her mother and how even Rita herself hadn't been enough to make her want to stay alive. By the time Rita had finished her solo, her shoulders were shaking, and she bowed her head, and I understood that she felt like an orphan and would for a long time thereafter. It was the feeling I had every time after a fight with my father, the fear that I was unloved. That was the look on Rita's face that night at the high school. Even though she was standing there with her mother, she kept glancing about as if, at any minute, she might run. I gave her a shy wave, just the slightest lifting of my hand, and she waved back, an exchange that both thrilled and shamed me because it was so secretive, so desperate, such a meager gesture in this time of our need.

That night, my parents and I approached a group of fathers. One of them, Mr. Albiero, was demonstrating his golf swing, and as we tried to pass, his arms came back and knocked off my father's hat. "Oh, I am sorry," he said. "Mr. Martin, please excuse me."

The bristles of my father's flat top hair cut had been mussed by the hat, and he looked a bit bewildered now. He unclasped his hooks and used one to push his eyeglasses up on his nose. He tipped back his head and squinted at Mr. Albiero. "Oh, Albiero," he said. "It's you."

My father had a habit of calling men by their last names, which seemed to me the wrong way to address someone, particularly people who called him "Mr. Martin."

"We were just talking golf," Mr. Albiero said. "I'm afraid I got carried away."

Larry was standing at the edge of the group. He picked up my father's hat, and I was ashamed that I hadn't done it first. My father opened his hook and stretched it out to Larry, who let my father take the hat by its brim. "Thank you, Little Albiero," he said, and again I felt that Larry was a better boy than I would ever be.

We had become friends in the fourth grade, brought together primarily by our shared love of sports, and though we were still friends in the eighth grade, it was becoming clear that we were different sorts of boys. He had become one of the popular crowd, a group of kids whose parents belonged to the same clubs and attended the same parties. My parents weren't joiners and never received invitations to social functions. Each summer, we left for the farm like migrant workers. It was never clear whether we meant to live in Oak Forest or whether we were just visiting. But now we had decided to stay, which meant that people wouldn't be able to ignore us as easily as they once had, and we wouldn't be able to keep to ourselves.

So when Mr. Albiero, feeling guilty, I suppose, about knocking off my father's hat, invited us to a graduation party at their house, my parents had no choice but to accept.

"That's very nice of you," my mother said. "Should I bring something?"

I imagined her coming into the Albiero's house with tupperware or something wrapped in aluminum foil, and I cringed.

"Oh, heavens, no," said Mr. Albiero as if it were the silliest notion in the world. "We're the hosts. We'll take care of everything."

As long as my father was alive, my mother carried a fork in her purse. Sometimes, after church, we would stop at a fast-food restaurant where the only eating utensils were plastic, and my father would need the fork in order to eat his hamburger and his french fries. It wasn't a pretty sight when he ate. He used the point of his left hook to pin his food to the plate and then the fork to tear away a piece. When he was finished, my mother had to clean his hooks with a napkin. He held them open for her so she could swab the insides of the prongs. He was proud of all he could do with his hooks. "Anything you can," he used to tell people, "except drink from a paper cup and wipe my ass." He could be crude that way, exhibit a roughness he had learned growing up on the farm. There, among men who labored in the fields and wrestled with machinery and doctored animals, he had no use for delicacy. It must have been impossible, even at a time of leisure to forget the coarse and brutal strength it took to castrate hogs, load cattle onto stock trucks, lift cultivators, heft seed sacks. Even after six years in Oak Forest, he carried this crudeness in the motions of his body—in his walk, more of a stomp, swift and purposeful, his arms swinging at his sides; in the way he knocked on a door, his hook pounding against the wood as if he were driving nails; in the way he ate those Sundays, tearing at his food the way I would later see him use his hooks to gut rabbits.

But there were times when he demonstrated a measure of elegance and grace. Sunday mornings, when my mother dressed him for church, he was particular about the trousers and shirts and jackets he wore. He considered colors and styles, often changed his mind, preened before the mirror until he was satisfied. He wasn't a religious man, but still he went with my mother and me to church. It must have given her some hope that one day the ugliness would ebb from our lives and we would be the sort of family who could walk into a church and not feel guilty for the fights and curses of the previous week. She had grown up trusting in God and her ability to endure anything with his help. She had been baptized as a young girl, and each Sunday, at communion, she broke off a bit from the cracker that represented Christ's broken body, and laid it on her tongue. She sipped grape juice from a dainty glass thimble—Christ's blood—and dabbed at her lips with a tissue. My father and I, because we weren't saved, never participated in communion. We were the lost souls the preacher implored to come forward and be saved, the ones for whom my mother surely must have prayed those nights when I saw her kneeling beside her bed the way her mother must have taught her years ago as a girl before she knew that one day she would marry my father and have a son and that, together, we would bring such misery to her life.

She was happiest on Sundays during that short time in church, where my father and I couldn't curse at each other, couldn't shout.

We were mute, and the only sounds were the hymns, the prayers, the whisper of Bible pages as they turned. Often, in the car on the drive home it would be awhile before any of us would speak, afraid, I imagine, to disturb the calm we had carried with us from the church.

One Sunday, Mr. Browning, the kinder of the two men who had visited us in our duplex five years before, asked my parents if he could drop by that afternoon for a chat. I knew what that meant; he wanted to convince my father to join the church. "Not today," my father said. "We're going to be gone this afternoon."

"Maybe some evening this week?" Mr. Browning said.

My father became more forceful. "You just want to tell me I'm going to hell. I don't need to listen to that."

In the car, my mother told him, "You could have been more polite."

"I could be a lot of things," he said, "but I'm not."

I doubt that she ever wished for another husband, though my father was often difficult and a burden to her. She was too loyal, had too much faith that people were essentially good, that goodness could save us. How could she believe anything else and live with my father and me? When she rode through the subdivisions and stared out her window at the grand homes with their elegant lawns, she must have thought, as we all surely did, that once we had one as our own, our lives would be more settled and kind.

Graduation was on a Friday evening. At the ceremony, I wore a white carnation pinned to my lapel and marched down the aisle that led through the audience to the temporary stage constructed on the school's asphalt playground. It was early evening, still plenty of daylight left, but the skies were overcast. The snapshots my mother took all have a bluish tint to them because she didn't use the flash. She was never adept with a camera, and, when I look at those snapshots now, they both amuse and sadden me. She never knew how to frame her subjects, so there's a shot of me holding my diploma where I'm without a head; only my torso appears. I could be any kid holding a diploma. There's another one, when I'm marching in, where my mother seems to have been focusing on the bare calf of the man sitting next to her, his trouser leg having crept up his shin. When I look at those pictures and recall those days, I'm convinced that my mother's intentions were good; she thought she had everything right where she wanted it.

Later that night, at Larry Albiero's graduation party, there was cake and ice cream and coffee and fruit punch. My mother was wearing a new dress and high heeled shoes. My father had on a black suit and a white shirt. The collar was loose, and I could see the white of his crew neck undershirt rising above the top button. Mr. Albiero wore a powder blue poplin suit and a light yellow necktie with tiny silver dots.

"What a glorious night," he said, as Mrs. Albiero prepared to cut the cake. We were all gathered around the dining table, which had been covered with a linen cloth.

Larry and I were standing next to each other, and I remember thinking that, if his father hadn't knocked off my father's hat that night at the high school and then felt guilty about it, we wouldn't even be in their house. We would be back in our apartment, and my father, wearing only his undershirt and boxer shorts, would be yawning and stretching and saying, as he often did when he was worn out, "Shit and two makes eight," a crude pun to signal the end of our day.

But here we were, in company that now felt strange to me. Larry, wearing a suit and necktie identical to his father's, seemed more capable and assured than I. He had told me, as we had shot a game of pool in his garage, that his father had gotten him a job as a caddy at his country club, the same country club that hosted a big shot PGA tournament. "I'll make a few bucks," he had said. "And contacts. That's what counts in the business world."

I knew nothing about golf, only that when I was a kid on the farm I had a set of plastic clubs and balls, and once when our cows got out and left hoof prints in our yard, I pretended they were holes and tried to hit the balls into them.

Before Mrs. Albiero served the cake, Mr. Albiero asked my father to say grace. It was a request that took my father by surprise, one made, I imagine, as a kindness, the way my mother, in later years, would often ask a guest to bless a meal. I feared that my father would snap at Mr. Albiero. My mother and I glanced at each other, and she looked as if she would speak, but just then, the doorbell rang, and Mr. Albiero excused himself so he could answer it.

When he returned, Rita Burns and her mother were with him. "Look who decided to come after all," he said. He was between Rita and her mother, a hand on each of their backs, as if it took this pressure to make them walk into the room. "God has certainly been glorious to bring us all here together tonight."

Mrs. Burns was a thin woman with drooping eyelids that fluttered as if she could hardly hold them open. Rita was wearing her hair in soft curls down the back of her long neck. The skin at her temples was very thin, and I could see the blue veins webbing beneath the surface. "Oh, look at the cake," Mrs. Burns said. "How lovely."

She reached out her hand toward the table, and her fingers were trembling. I thought of how desperately someone could want something and never have it come true. Still, there were moments such as these when a woman who had nearly killed herself could walk into a room and look at a cake as if it were the bread of Heaven, and my parents and I, who watched, could know how starved we were, how lost, blindly trying to feel our way home.

Come mid-summer, we would leave Oak Forest for good and move back to our farm. "City people," my father would say with a smirk whenever someone would ask him why we had come back. "They're always nosing around in your business."

EIGHT

Our farmhouse, when we returned to it in the summer of 1969, was run-down and out-of-date. Even my mother, who rarely complained about anything, made it known that, if we were to live there, we would have to bring the house up to speed. We would have to install indoor plumbing, and put down new linoleum, and patch the crumbling plaster in the walls, and lower the high ceilings, and do something about the roof that let water leak into a bedroom closet. She started a list, her pen moving with ease across a writing tablet:

Plumbing
Linoleum
Walls
Ceilings
Roof

My father and I sat at the kitchen table, watching. "That's going to take some cash," he said. He tipped back his head and looked up at the ceiling. Then he looked down at his hooks, which he had clasped by their points on the kitchen table. "I'm not sure the old place is worth it. We could look around. Maybe Sumner."

"Buy a house." My mother tapped her pen against the writing tablet. "Move again."

"Ten miles," said my father. "That shouldn't be too rough."

As always, he had his own ideas. If we stayed on the farm, he told me, I'd go to Bridgeport High School. I'd have to ride the bus, and, during basketball season, someone would have to drive into town to pick me up after practices and games. "You'd be a country kid," he told me, "and that makes it hard. I can promise you that." The country kids rarely went out for sports. They joined the Future Farmers of America and got part-time jobs through the school's vocational program. "When you're a country kid," he said, "people have a certain idea of you. They think you're a bumpkin. But you didn't just fall off the hay wagon. You're no rube. You'll show them you're sharper than what they think."

He had been one of the country kids. He had risen early to do his morning chores and then made the trip into Sumner, catching rides with other country kids who drove their families' Model T's. When school was over, he came straight back to the farm so he could help my grandfather with the evening milking and feeding. By this time, my aunts were both married, and my father was alone on the farm with my grandparents and no one—like my Aunt Lucille or Aunt Ruth—was there to buffer the rough edges that often rubbed between my father and my grandfather. Will Martin would have been sixty by then, set in his ways. I imagine he had little patience with my father, the youngest of his children. My grandfather had lost too much and lived too long to indulge anyone who was reckless and devil-may-care. In the few photographs I have of him, there is a sad, stunned look on his face. His lips turn down at the corners, and his eyes stare off past the camera as if he's looking at something only he can see. There is a cleft in his weak chin that makes it seem he's close to crying. It's as if he knows he can't trust his life. There he is, in a studio shot, posing with Ella, his first wife, and their two children, Glen and Mae. He's sitting on a kitchen chair, wearing the best suit of clothes he owns. His hands are on his legs, and his wife and children are touching him. Glen, standing to his right, grips his wrist. Mae, to his left, puts her hand on his. Ella, behind Mae, lays her hand on his shoulder. The photograph foreshadows something ominous. Ella is wearing a black dress, and she stands slightly removed from the rest of the family. Her left arm is straight, her hand stretched out, the fingers rigid. Soon she'll be a victim of an outbreak of influenza, and her death, when it occurs, will make my life possible. Her leaving the world will cause my grandfather, a year later, to marry my grandmother Martin who will give birth to my father, who will say to me, that summer of 1969, "You don't want to be a country kid. Trust me."

He had always imagined that he knew what was best for me, as I suspect his father did for him. For once, I agreed. I *didn't* want to be a country kid, hemmed in by the farm as my father had been when he was my age. During the six years we had spent in Oak Forest, I had started to experience how large the world was, and to return to those eighty acres, sectioned off and lined with fences, seemed unacceptable to me. So, when we went to Sumner to look at houses, I was excited. My mother and father seemed to be as well. My mother had put on bright red lipstick, which she rarely did, and my father had changed from his olive-green work suit to a silver-gray sport shirt and a pair of navy blue trousers. He was wearing the belt with the initial, "M," on the buckle. I had given it to him on Father's Day, and seeing it now, glittering in the brilliant sunshine, made me think this was the start of something. We were moving to Sumner, starting over. "What a day," he said, as we drove past the field where he had lost his hands. "Nothing but blue skies." He tapped my knee with his hook. "Hey, Buster Brown? Doesn't it make you glad you're alive?"

I told him that it did.

"Damn straight it does." He tooted the horn. "You'd have to be a fool to feel blue on a day like this."

My mother was sitting in the backseat, not saying a word. She was staring out her window at the farmland she had seen a million times, flat pastures of timothy and clover, fields of soybeans and corn, golden stretches of wheat, but still there was a bright look on her face, expectant, as if she thought she might see something new. No matter how miserable my father and I made her life, she always had faith that the next day would be better. "Time takes care of everything," she was fond of saying. Still, on this day, I wonder whether she doubted my father, thought his impulse to buy a house in Sumner another drastic attempt to land us on stable ground. It had been his decision to leave Oak Forest after that night at Larry Albiero's graduation party, and my mother had agreed to it. She had retired from teaching after thirty-eight years, had given up that part of herself. Perhaps she was ready to step away from the classroom. As the years had gone on, her third graders had become more and more difficult for her to endure. Those last days in Oak Forest, she had seemed weary and frazzled. There had been complaints from parents that she let her class get unruly. The school board had debated asking for her resignation before finally deciding to offer her a contract. For years and years, she had been trying to please everyone around her. She had suffered my father's demands, the tension he and I brought into her life, the squabbling parents, the fragile students, the demanding principals and superintendents. She had earned a rest.

"I want flower beds," she said from the backseat.

My father glanced up in the rearview mirror. "Flower beds," he said.

"That's right," said my mother. "Wherever we buy a house, I want there to be lots and lots of flowers."

* * *

The house we bought was a one-story frame house covered with white clapboards. It was an old house that had been remodeled by the seller, a Mr. Murray, who lived in the house next to it. He had bought the house and remodeled it for his newly married daughter and her husband, but they had decided to live in a trailer park on the edge of town.

"Now, I've got this house, see?" Mr. Murray said as he worked the key into the knob on the front door. He owned a welding shop uptown. He was tall and thin and wore a pair of coveralls and a hat that looked like a train engineer's. He smoked a pipe with a shiny steel stem, and his mouth stretched out to the side as he spoke in a laconic drawl. "It's a pretty good house. Someone ought to have it. You say you folks come from up around Chicago?"

"We've been up there the last six years," my father said. "My wife was teaching school, but we're from Lukin Township. I've got a farm down there on the county line."

"County line, you say?" Mr. Murray turned the key in the lock. "I do some welding not too far from there for a fella named Homer Read."

"That's my brother," my mother said.

"Well, you don't say. Why, sure I know Homer. He's a pretty good old boy." Mr. Murray turned the knob and pushed open the door. "Go on in," he said. "Give the place a look. I'll be out here on the porch if you want to know anything."

There were three bedrooms, a living room, a dining room, a kitchen and a bath. I remember the smell of fresh varnish on the hardwood floors, the light blue paint on the front bedroom's walls, the window in the living room that looked out onto the side porch and on up the street, into the shade of the spreading oak trees that lined it.

"You'd only be a block from school," my father said to me. "How handy is that?"

"Handy," I said.

"You bet it is."

My mother opened closets and peered inside. She stepped into the kitchen, a rectangular room at the rear of the house, and saw the ample cabinets. There were decorative wrought iron rods that ran from the bottoms of the cabinets to the counter top. The rods had rings, about three inches across, screwed into them.

"What in the world do you think these are?" my father said.

"Flower pots." My mother ran her finger around one of the rings. "I could put flower pots here."

Outside, Mr. Murray showed us the lot. "Actually, you've got two lots here. The property goes back to that fence line."

On the other side of the fence was nothing but space, a field of grass and weeds that stretched all the way to the railroad tracks. I could see the stone of the trestle gleaming in the sun.

"Plenty of room for a garden," my father said.

"Oh, you could do a garden here, all right," said Mr. Murray. "Put up a basketball hoop for the boy if you're a mind to. Do you like basketball, son?"

"Yes, sir."

"Why sure. I figured you might."

We had looked at only a few houses—there weren't that many for sale in a town of twelve hundred people—and I favored a newer ranch-style home at the edge of town. It had a recreation room with a fireplace, and I had already started to imagine the friends I had yet to make gathering there to listen to records or watch television. Maybe I'd even get a billiard table like Larry Albiero. But now Mr. Murray, with his easy-going style and his friendly gab, was winning me, as he was my parents. He was the good neighbor we had seen in numerous television shows, the kind father who would remodel a house for his daughter and not even complain when she decided she didn't want it. He was, and this thought surprised me and left me feeling guilty for knowing it, the sort of man my mother deserved to marry.

"So what's your asking price?" My father's voice went hard, the way it often did when he did business, on guard for anyone who might try to cheat him.

"I was thinking ten thousand dollars." Mr. Murray lifted one leg and bent over to tap out his cold pipe on his boot heel. "What about you? Do you think that's fair?"

"What about the interest rate?"

"Oh, I don't need any interest."

"No interest?"

"Neighbor, the way I figure it, Uncle Sam's just going to tax it and get the most of it in the end. Better that you have it. You're good folks. I can tell that."

Mr. Murray smiled, and it was as if he were blessing us there at the start of our new life. All thoughts of the ranch-style house with the recreation room vanished from my mind. "Good folks," he had called us. I knew the deal was as good as done.

My father told the story again and again, the one about John Murray and what a decent fellow he was to refuse to ask for interest on the mortgage of the house. "That's someone you can count on," my father said. "We couldn't ask for a better neighbor."

Later that day, we drove back into town so I could take a snapshot of the house with my Polaroid camera. When I look at the photograph now, I see the creases at the corners where my father clamped it between the prongs of his hook as he took it from his shirt pocket to show to people. "That's our house," he said. "Lee took the picture with his camera. Dang thing develops right there in front of your eyes. Now how do you like that?"

Once more, my father was cheerful, my mother more relaxed, and I, for a change, looked forward to each morning, when my father said, "Rise and shine, buddy. It's time to get to work."

We moved furniture from our farm into town and started to put together our new house. We brought three beds, two nightstands, a chest of drawers, a desk, a dining table, a coffee table, lamps, the rocking chair that had been my Grandma Martin's. When I lifted it by the arms, I felt the smooth surface where her hands had worried the wood for years.

What we didn't have, we bought. We made trips to Olney and Vincennes and wandered through furniture and appliance stores. At my father's insistence, we bought a dresser, a desk, and a bookcase for my room. We bought a green living room suite: a sofa, two easy chairs, an ottoman, and a recliner. My father tried out the recliner in the store. The salesclerk showed him how to operate the lever that brought up the footrest. My father laid back in the chair. "Now that's living," he said.

We bought a refrigerator and a stove. "What color should we get?" my mother said. "White?"

"No, get the avocado," I told her.

"Avocado," she said with a laugh. "You don't think that's showy?"

"Get it," my father said. "It's an eye-catcher."

My mother looked at the price tag. "But it's more expensive."

"Money," my father told her. "We're saving a bundle on interest. So who's counting?"

We bought a painting to hang above our new sofa. It was a farm scene: a red barn surrounded by a rail fence, shaded by tall trees, a pasture stretching back to the horizon. "I like that," my father said, and it was ours.

There were other boys in our new neighborhood, but I was too shy to make myself known to them. I stood at the windows, hiding myself in the folds of the draperies, as I spied on their comings and goings. My father went out and talked to our neighbors and brought back reports. The Moan family across the street had three sons. One of them, Neal, was my age. He was a skinny kid with black hair that hung down in his eyes. His father drove a tank truck for the Texaco oil refinery, and it was Neal's job, while Mr. Moan was on the road, to keep their lawn in shape. I watched him, when I knew he couldn't see me, and I admired the way he could work on a lawn mower, handling wrenches and screwdrivers, knowing exactly what to do to keep the machine running. I saw him dismantle the carburetor to clean it, remove the blade and carry it away on his bicycle (to Mr. Murray's welding shop, I assumed) to get it sharpened. He had a red shop rag he kept in his hip pocket, and from time to time, he used it to wipe grease from his hands or to clean a spark plug or to hold the crankcase's dipstick as he eyed the oil level. I had never been mechanically inclined, a source of constant frustration for my father, who expected my help on the farm, and Neal Moan seemed so expert that I envied him. He moved with the confidence that comes from having lived long enough in a place to get the idea you own it. He mowed lawns for other people in town, and I saw him ride his bicycle down alley ways, pulling his mower behind him, knowing the short cuts that would take him where he needed to go.

My parents encouraged me to go out sometime when Neal was around and introduce myself.

"I wouldn't know what to say," I told them.

"Just tell him who you are," my father said. "You can say your name, can't you? That's not hard."

Not for him, but I was shy like my mother. "It might be scary at first." She gave me a sympathetic smile. "It always is when you're new. But if you don't make the effort, you'll be lonely."

I imagined that my mother had been lonely a long time before she had met my father. I thought she would probably make the same choice again because it seemed human nature to me for people to come together no matter what it might cost. I longed for Neal Moan to know me because he seemed so certain of his place in this town while I was the new kid, anxious to be a part of what went on there.

So one evening toward dusk, when I was riding my bicycle down our street and Neal was on the sidewalk in front of his house, crouched down by his mower, I stopped and said, as my father had advised, "I'm Lee."

He lifted his head and squinted through his shaggy bangs. "Neal," he said.

"I've seen you mowing," I told him.

He took the red shop rag from his hip pocket and swiped it over the engine housing. "Yeah."

The worst thing I could imagine was happening. We had absolutely nothing to talk about.

"Well, I'll see you," I said.

I got my bicycle turned around and started to pedal away. Then Neal said, "Hey," and I stopped and circled back. "I know where there's some beer," he said. "You drink beer, don't you?"

"Sure," I said, even though it wasn't true.

I followed him down the alley behind his house and ended up at the garage beside the neighborhood grocery. It was a rickety garage, and Neal pushed aside one of the planks so we could squeeze through. A car sat inside, and Neal opened the back door. He ducked down, and I heard the squeak of a styrofoam cooler. Then he reached something back to me, and I took two bottles in my hands and felt the water on the glass. "We'll leave something for next time," he said. Then we slipped back into the alley, and as easily as that, I learned to be a thief.

* * *

The next day, I had to go to the high school for my sports physical. Baseball practice would start that afternoon, and my father had already made it clear that he expected me to go out for the team.

"I don't want to," I told him.

"Did you hear that?" he said to my mother. We were sitting at our new chrome-edged dinette set eating breakfast. "He doesn't want to play baseball."

My mother, to my surprise, was wearing a pair of slacks. It was the first time I had seen her in anything but a dress, and I thought how odd it was. The slacks made her seem impulsive, someone I could no longer trust. "I thought you liked baseball," she said to me.

I did, but not the way I loved basketball. I had never played little league because we left Oak Forest each summer and arrived on the farm long after league play had started in Sumner. Therefore, I had little confidence in my skills, which had only been proven in sandlot games, and the thought of putting myself on display in front of kids I didn't know terrified me. To my father, though, I was just being difficult. I was throwing a monkey wrench into the new life he had planned for us. Only days before he had come home from the barber shop all hepped up because he had run into one of the school's star athletes, Kenny King, and had told him all about me—what an arm I had, how I could really spank the ball.

"He's expecting you," my father said. "I told him you were a crackerjack."

"But I don't know anyone," I said.

"You'll know Kenny. Just tell him you're Roy Martin's boy."

Years before, when I was five, my parents took me into Sumner and left me at the high school for the Kiwanis Club Christmas cartoons. "Your dad will be back to get you," my mother said. "Go on. Have a good time." I sat on the bleachers with town kids I didn't know. They were all chattering away with one another, and I sat there, afraid to look around, afraid to move, for fear someone would notice me, or worse yet, say something to me, and then I would have to answer. I was thankful when the lights went out, and the movies started. I watched Chilly Willy and Woody Woodpecker and Tom and Jerry. Then the lights came up, and we all filed out of the gymnasium. At the door, men from the Kiwanis Club were passing out paper bags full of Christmas candy. I clutched mine, feeling that some mistake had been made since I was an impostor, not a town kid at all. I stepped out into the cold. The sidewalk was slushy with melting snow. Kids were tromping through the playground, running down the street, their laughter echoing. I looked all around for my parents, but they were nowhere to be seen. I stood there in the dim light, my face tingling with cold, while other kids got into warm cars or started the walk toward home. How long was I to wait? My mother had said my father would come back for me. Had he finally seen his chance to escape his miserable son? I walked uptown and went into the first store I recognized, the dime store where I often pleaded for toys. I had always been a selfish kid, and now I was convinced I was paying for all the times I had thrown tantrums. "Have you seen my dad?" I asked the salesclerk. He was a bald man who wore a string cowboy tie. "Who's your dad?" he asked. I said my father's name, "Roy Martin," and then I heard the bell on the door jingle. When I turned around, there was my father as if my saying his name had conjured him out of the air. "You should have seen how big your eyes got," he said every time he told the story over the years. "Yes, sir. At least once in your life you were glad to see your old man."

I remembered all that the morning I stepped inside the high school for my sports physical. I went through the same doors I had gone through the day of the Christmas cartoons. The cartoons had ended a few minutes before my father had thought they would, and by the time he got there to pick me up, I had started my walk uptown. He had seen me trudging up Main Street, and had parked the car and followed me to the dime store. Always, I had thought that he had some sort of special eminence in town because of his hooks. People were always holding doors open for him; when he paid bills in stores, the clerks took his wallet from his shirt pocket and removed the bills they needed. Everyone knew him and seemed to like him, and on the day I had thought I was lost, he had appeared and rescued me. Now I imagined that, as he had assured me, if I told people I was his son, some sort of special dispensation would fall on me.

The first thing I did inside the high school was duck into the rest room to comb my hair. There, standing in front of the mirror, was Kenny King, running a comb over his thick sideburns. He was a senior, and I knew who he was because my father had made a big deal of pointing him out to me over the years. He was the star athlete, the golden boy, the town's pride. The fact that he was the first person I saw inside the school seemed like a good omen to me, and, buoyed by this good fortune, I said to him, "You're Kenny," which sounded silly as soon as I said it because, of course, he knew who he was.

He eyed me in the mirror, but didn't say anything in response.

"My dad's Roy Martin," I said.

"Roy Martin." He slipped his comb into his hip pocket. "That old blowhard. Yeah, he was going on about you the other day at the barber shop. You must think you're a real hotshot."

"No," I said, backing out of the rest room. "I'm no hotshot."

For the first time, it was clear to me that my father didn't exert as much influence as I had always imagined. The fact was there were people like Kenny King who thought him haughty and ridiculous. I felt embarrassed for my father, who had only meant to make things easier for me, but I was angry, too, because, thanks to his boasting, my life in Sumner promised to be harder and more precarious than I had at first thought.

When I got home from my physical, my Grandma Read was there. She had come to stay with us for a while. Her health was failing, and she had given up her home in Berryville, living instead with first one child and then another. Her hearing aid whistled, and she reached up to adjust its volume. Once, when my father was driving over a gravel road after a grader had made a ridge in the center, and the rocks were spraying the chassis and making such a racket, my grandmother merely reached up and turned down her hearing aid and then sat there with a content smile on her face. I envied the way she was able to shut out the din, a trick I wished I could perform every time my father and I began to shout at each other.

"Well, how do you like your new house?" Grandma Read laid her hand on my arm, and I felt her trembling fingers. "Does it suit you?"

She had palsy in her hands, and, when she touched me, I thought of the shaky scrawl of her handwriting, so much like my father's in the letters he had written my mother from Barnes Hospital in St. Louis where he had been learning to use his hooks.

"It's all right," I said.

"And your father says you're going to play baseball. That's fine. Your Grandpa Read always liked baseball. What position will you play?"

"I don't know," I said. Then I ducked into my room, the flutter of her fingers still alive on my skin.

I was at that age where people I had loved all my life suddenly became suspect for no better reason than the fact that they thought they knew what was best for me. Across the country, it was a time of rebellion. Even in the seemingly placid midwest, college students had begun to protest the Vietnam War. Young men burned their draft cards. They burned American flags. Young women joined them in sit-ins and demonstrations. Within the year, National Guardsmen would kill four students at Kent State University in Ohio. Southern Illinois University in Carbondale would close because of antiwar demonstrations. There would be violent confrontations between students, police, and Guardsmen. A curfew would go into effect, as would a ban on the sale of gasoline in containers, liquor, and ammunition. People like my father said the world was going to hell in a handbasket all because of the goddamned long-haired hippies. If boys wanted to look like girls, he said, someone ought to cut off their peckers.

The truth was I wanted to let my hair grow, wear bell-bottomed blue jeans and sandals and leather vests. My father assured me that would never happen, not as long as I put my feet under his table, and besides, as soon as basketball season started I would have to adhere to the dress code that dictated that no hair would touch the shirt collar or the tops of the ears or fall over the forehead in bangs. That morning at the school physical, I had seen a sign in the locker room that said, *Look Sharp! Dress Sharp! Be a Winner!* Even a star like Kenny King would have to lose his glorious sideburns since the code dictated that they be no longer than the higher notch of the ear.

Though Sumner was, in many ways, a sleepy, backwoods town, young people there weren't immune to the wider world. The resistance to authority that we saw each night on the evening news, read about in the newspaper, heard in rock music, appealed to us as much as it did the teenagers in New York, Chicago, San Francisco. We heard the messages: "Tune in, Turn on, Drop out," "Make Love, Not War," "Don't Trust Anyone over Thirty."

Perhaps I was particularly receptive to this era of defiance because, for so long, I had lived under my father's strict rule. What he couldn't understand, was that every time he had whipped me—

every time he had raised his voice to bully me—I had taken the lash of his belt, the scathing bite of his tongue deep inside where rage and contempt festered and waited for the opportunity to return.

That afternoon, when my mother called me from my room to lunch, I had already made up my mind that, no matter what my father said, I wasn't going to go to baseball practice.

"You *are* going," my father told me. "Mister, you just better get used to that idea."

It was especially painful for me to deny him because sports had always been the one thing we had shared. Through all the ugliness between us, we had always found that common ground, whether it was baseball or basketball or even something as ludicrous as professional wrestling, and now, with my refusal, I was taking that restorative away from us.

I wished it could be otherwise. I watched my father hold a glass of iced tea between the prongs of his hook, and I feared, as I always did, that the glass would shatter, though it never had. He drank from the glass. Then, he set it on the table and tried to let it go, but, as often happened, he couldn't get the hook to open wide enough to allow the glass to come free. I saw his shoulder muscles straining, heard the steel joints of his harness squeaking beneath his shirt. "I'm fast," he said, as he always did with an air of resignation whenever his hooks had bound him to something.

My mother reached over and took the glass. My father's hook snapped shut. Then there was a long silence in our house, punctuated only by the sounds of my mother laying her knife on her plate and my grandmother rustling her paper napkin. I had my head bowed, but I could tell that my father was glaring at me.

I remembered a day, years before, when I had asked him to play ball. It was always my mother who hit fly balls to me, who played catch, and I wanted, just once, to know what it would be like to have my father do these things. To my surprise, he agreed. It was late evening, nearly dark, and we were in the front yard on our farm. I could hear locusts chirring in the trees, and our voices echoing in the still air. My bat was a Roger Maris autograph model, a Louisville Slugger of blond ash. My father gripped the handle between his hooks and took his stance. I lobbed the baseball to him underhand, and he swung. Even now, in my memory, I can hear the crack of the bat against the ball, can see the arc of the ball's flight, a pop-up I settled under and caught. "Do it again," I said, and my father obliged. I pitched and he hit until it was too dark to see the ball. I'm not sure whether I've ever been happier than I was that night. Then, when he finally dropped the bat, and I picked it up, I felt the rough wood, splintered from where his hooks had gouged it. "I'm sorry," he said, when I showed it to him. "I guess we just didn't think."

What was he thinking that day at lunch, when I told him I wouldn't go to baseball practice? That I was betraying him? That he had brought us to this house in Sumner where Mr. Murray had painted the walls, refinished the wood floors, left ornamental wrought iron rings on the counters for my mother's flower pots, only to have me spoil our hopes for a decent, regular life?

My Grandma Read's hearing aid started whistling, a high-pitched keening like the emergency broadcast system signal that occasionally disrupted a television program. "This is a test of the emergency broadcast system," an announcer's voice always said. "It is only a test."

My grandma turned down her hearing aid, and my father said to me, "I told Kenny King all about you." He said it with a note of pleading in his voice. I heard it. I can't deny I took it inside me. It felt familiar because it was the same yearning I had experienced every time I had hid myself behind the folds of the drapes and watched Neal Moan and the other neighborhood boys and had wished for the courage to join them. All his life, my father would be the country kid, eager for some semblance of a more perfect life that would always elude him. On that day, in 1969, when we were making our new start, I was his best hope, and I turned against him.

"Kenny King says you're a blowhard," I said.

"A blowhard?" said my father. "Why that little prick."

I knew I had hurt him, and I knew I had meant to, as surely as Neal Moan had slipped into the garage beside the neighborhood grocery and stolen two bottles of beer. At the time, it had seemed like such a harmless act, but now, seeing how much I had hurt my father, I realized how little it took to make a life something impossible to contain. I didn't know yet all that would happen to us during the years we would spend in our new house, but I felt some splendor go off the shiny floors, the freshly painted walls, the gleaming avocado refrigerator and range. Through the kitchen window, I could see Mr. Murray, home from his shop for lunch, strolling though his garden. A wisp of smoke trailed off from his pipe, as he bent to balance a ripening tomato on his palm. I imagined the swell of the fruit, the weight, how he must have been gauging how long it would be before the tomato would be ready to pick. He thought he had judged us correctly. "You're good folks," he had said.

"Are you going?" my father asked me.

My grandmother was smiling at me. Having her there made all of this worse because she was about to see how terrible my father and I could be to each other.

"I'm not going," I said.

My father banged his hooks together. The steel rang out, a clanging that carried out into the air. I saw Mr. Murray lift his head. I imagined him making the ornamental wrought iron rings on which my mother's flower pots rested. I saw him heating the iron, patiently bending the line of it into a circle, imagining his daughter and how she would live there next to him, live there for years and years in a house he had made new.

"I'm not going," I said again, and I didn't.

NINE

My mother grew irises and daffodils, peonies and naked ladies. We had a lilac bush beside the house in Sumner that filled the air each spring with its sweet perfume. In the backyard, my father put in apple trees, peach trees, a cherry bush. Along the back of the garden, he transplanted blackberry and raspberry briars from the farm, planted rhubarb, put in a bed of strawberries. The garden itself was lush each year with the tall pyramids of pole beans, the sprawling tendrils of cucumber vines, the fat gourds of white long-necked squash. We grew corn, tomatoes, peas, lettuce, carrots, beets, broccoli, cauliflower, potatoes, green peppers. Nothing was beyond my father's gardening skills, not eggplant or cantaloupe or water-melon or parsnips. Nothing gave him more joy than to stroll through the garden each evening, checking on its progress. Often, he stood at the wire fence that separated our property from the Murrays' and gabbed awhile with Mr. Murray until my mother told me to call my father into supper. He came in, chuckling over some story Mr. Murray had told him, and we sat at our table, a cool breeze lifting the curtains at the windows, and we were happy.

We were happy on Sunday afternoons that fall when we went for long drives in the country to look at the trees, ablaze with or-ange and red and yellow. The sunlight was so warm it was tempting to imagine that winter might never come. And when it finally did, we were content on cold nights to pop corn and pare apples and sit at our kitchen table, the radio on so we could listen to a basketball game. Each morning, I woke to that same radio playing softly, always the same commercial at six-thirty—a woman's voice crooning, calling me up from sleep, "And like a good neighbor, State Farm is there." I was happy to hear my mother moving about in the kitchen, to smell bacon frying and coffee perking, to listen to the roar of the gas heating stove coming on in the dining room. I stood in front of it in my pajamas and let the warmth spread across my back while I watched the morning brighten outside our window. I could see the hoar frost, white on the ground, could hear the bare branches of trees clacking in the wind, and, even though I knew I would soon have to step out into that cold and make my way to school, I was thankful because my mother was in their bedroom now helping my father dress, and I knew we had all made it through another night. I gave thanks because I had started to realize how my parents were aging (my mother was fifty-nine; my father, fifty-six), and my biggest fear was that one or both of them would die.

For some reason, this fear was strongest at Christmas, perhaps because each year it seemed that we heard about disaster finding a family during the holidays. A house would burn or someone would die unexpectedly, and I would start to believe it could happen to us, and then it would be other people saying, "Those poor Martins. Did you hear?"

Still, each Christmas, we went into the woods on our farm and cut a cedar tree to stand before the side window in our living room and decorate with tinsel and ornaments and lights as if we had all the confidence in the world that we would stay healthy and safe. My father brought home paper sacks full of hard candy, chocolate drops, nuts, and if we thought anything at all about the time he had bought too much and my mother and I had left it for the Sidebottoms, we never mentioned it. We had travelled so far since then—to Oak Forest and back—and now we were cozy in our new home and trying hard, no matter the sharp words that sometimes flared up between us, to forge a more respectful way of living.

We tacked up lights around our front porch, wrapped the columns with red ribbon, listened to carols on the radio, hid presents from one another. My father made sure I always got the one extravagant gift I requested each year: a barbell set, a portable typewriter, an archery set, a shotgun. He bought me the record albums I asked for, though they meant nothing to him but the noise they would make on my stereo. Each year, I opened my gifts on Christmas morning and sat there, amazed that my father, who had never told me he loved me—had never kissed me or hugged me or touched me with affection—had been so generous.

He had forgiven me for not playing baseball. My mother was right—time did have a way of healing our wounds, or at least scabbing them over. Basketball season started, and I was on the freshman-sophomore team and the junior varsity. My father, when he wasn't seeing to something on the farm, spent winter afternoons loafing in the barber shop, the pool hall, still boasting about my athletic skills. He and my mother came to my games and sat in the bleachers with the other parents, all of them younger. My mother kept a tally of how many points each player scored in a pocket-sized note pad. My father joined the other fathers in jeering at the referees: "Open your eyes." "Call a foul." "Get him a saddle, ref. He's riding him." My parents drove to all of the away games, even to the farthest town, Enfield, which was a seventy-five mile trip over narrow, two-lane blacktops. Sometimes, it would be close to midnight when I got back on the team bus, but my parents would be waiting up for me, and we would have a snack and talk about the games. My father bragged about the good plays I had made. My mother showed me the scorecard she had kept. And for a while, we forgot about the cold night outside, and the earth turning on its axis, and how late it really was.

Then, one day, I saw David Sidebottom. It was Saturday, and I was cutting across the school yard on my way home from the barber shop. The cold air stung the back of my neck where the barber had shaved the short hairs. On the asphalt basketball court, a group of grade school kids had a game going. In their midst, was a tall, burly boy, and when he turned so I could see his face, I knew it was David. He had taken off his coat, despite the cold day, and he was wearing a T-shirt with holes in it, a pair of blue jeans, patched at the knees, and a pair of work boots, the laces undone, the tongues lolling. He held the basketball high above his head, and the grade-schoolers, most of them wearing sock hats, jumped and jumped, laughing because they knew there wasn't a chance in the world that they would ever reach that ball. David knew it, too, and he laughed along with them, not in a mean way—not like a bully—but with joy, the way a father or an older brother might chuckle while horsing around with boys who were dear to him.

After that day at school, when David had kicked me, and my teacher had made me return the punishment, my friends and I had treated him horribly. He had laughed at me when I had tapped him with my soft-toed sneakers, and my friends were eager to make him pay. Though I went along with them, I can honestly say I regretted my involvement even at the time our abuse was taking place. We shoved him down during games on the playground, chose him last for our teams, refused to sit next to him on the school bus. To the shame of all of us who persecuted him, he was cheerful through it all. No matter what we did, he grinned, as if he had determined that he would never show how much our badgering actually hurt him. At the school picnic in the state park, we took him off into the woods and made him strip down to his underpants. He obliged with that irrepressible grin we had come to know. He seemed truly amused at how far we would go to humiliate him. We made off with his clothes, and he had to walk out of the woods and back to the shelter house, nearly naked. Not long after that, his family moved away, and, for years, the last image I had of him, was one of a little boy trudging out of the woods, wearing only his white underpants and a silly grin.

He was a little boy, no longer. He was taller than me and broader across the shoulders. He was raw-boned and had matinee-idol good looks: smooth, brown skin; black hair; icy blue eyes. When he tried to shoot the basketball, he flung it—no touch, only strength—and it slammed off the backboard and caromed over to where I was standing.

The laughter, which had been bubbling up into the cold air, stopped. The grade school kids stuffed their hands into their coat pockets. David kicked at the asphalt with the toe of his boot. He was sheepish now because he knew I had caught him playing a merry game with kids half his age, not for the appreciation of the sport, but for the pure joy.

I was standing to the side, perhaps twenty-five feet from the basket. I let go with a jump shot, the ball spinning perfectly off my finger tips. David and the grade school kids watched the high arc of the ball. Out of the corner of my eye, I saw my father's truck pull to the curb. The ball reached its apex and began its descent toward the basket. My father honked his horn. I stood there watching the ball, my arm still uplifted from the motion of the shot, my wrist bent in a perfect follow-through. There is always that moment, for a pure shooter, when he knows the ball is going in the basket—something about the weight of the ball, the distance, the spin and arc. I knew. And I knew that when the ball finally swished through the net, dead center so there would only be the sound of the leather rippling the cords, it would shame David Sidebottom. My father had got out of his truck and was calling my name. I walked toward him, hearing, finally, the ball zipping through the net and bouncing, once, twice, on the asphalt before someone grabbed it. Then one of the grade school kids said, "Wow," in hushed admiration, not knowing that I was the villain, the one who had just shown up a boy who wanted nothing more than a few moments of gleeful play on a winter Saturday.

As my father and I drove away, I saw David throwing the ball at the basket again and again, throwing it hard, like it was a baseball. The backboard rattled with the force. I had never heard a single sound that cried out with so much rage unless it was the sound of my father's hooks banging together just before he took off his belt to whip me. The grade school kids backed away from David. It was the last time I ever saw him so I have no idea what he finally did with his rage or what consequences it brought to his life.

"Who's that boy?" my father said.

I remembered the evening David's father had come to our farm to ask for work, and my father had turned him away.

"Just a boy," I said. An angry boy, I thought. Someone like me.

Many years before, my Sunday school teacher, Miss Kate, had called me a "bad boy," and now, after the incident with David on the playground, I feared it might be true. In Oak Forest, I had witnessed Bob Lahr's rage. I had been in Sumner the night when Jack Brian had killed his father. Now that I lived there, I was seeing that there were boys who were always in trouble. They broke into stores, stole cars, beat each other with tire irons, cut each other with knives. And though by every appearance I was more decent—one of the jocks, an honor-roll student—I started to suspect that like the ones my father called juvenile delinquents, I had an evil heart.

The summer between my freshman and sophomore year, I fell

in with a boy named Steve Vernon. It was rock music that first brought us together. We worked that summer for the Dekalb Seed Company, detassling corn. All day, we walked down rows and rows of corn, pulling out the tassel from each female stalk so the male stalks could pollinate them. We disappeared into the green corn, the tassels usually higher than our heads, and on our passes down the long fields, we might only glimpse the boy in the row next to us. We might only hear the whisk of the broad leaves, the snap of the tassel being pulled. We operated in six-man crews, and Steve Vernon was the boy who worked the row next to mine.

One day, I heard him singing. The song was *Spinning Wheel* by Blood, Sweat & Tears. He was singing under his breath in a sweet, thin tenor voice: "What goes up, must come down."

I joined him: "Spinnin' wheel got to go 'round."

Then we stopped. I could hear the other boys tromping down the rows. The corn leaves parted in front of me, and there was Steve. He was wearing an Army shirt with the sleeves cut out, a peace symbol medallion on a chain around his neck. He had prominent cheekbones, and curly hair he would later pick into an afro, persisting with that style despite the ugly name some of the other boys would coin for him: "Nigger Knots."

"It's Your Thing," he said, and then raised his eyebrows. I realized he was quizzing me to see whether I knew the artist.

"Isley Brothers," I told him.

"Light My Fire," he said.

"José Feliciano."

"Or?"

"The Doors."

He gave a nod of his head and then ducked back into his own row. He started singing *Reach Out of the Darkness*, and I tried to harmonize with him.

I don't recall whose idea it was to start stealing record albums, but I imagine it was mine. For a while, I had been thinking about taking insignificant items from people's homes, things I had no interest in owning, for the simple reason that I wanted some way to disturb what I imagined to be the smug security of lives lived in other houses. Of course, I didn't know anything about my motivations then. I only knew that I kept thinking about the night Neal Moan and I had stolen those two bottles of beer and the great pleasure it gave me to imagine the owner of that car coming out to the garage to retrieve his cooler. He would count and recount, trying to remember whether he had drunk two more bottles than he could recall. He would scratch his head, and an unnerving chill would pass into him, the thought that someone had been there; someone had been inside his car. I wanted to be that chill, that shiver, that heart-rattling moment when someone knew that nothing we imagine ours is safe. I fell asleep at night, dreaming the instant when one of my aunts might reach for a saltshaker, or one of my friend's father might open a drawer for his lighter fluid and find it gone.

That autumn, when cool weather had come, I went into stores and slipped record albums under my coat. I did it when I was with Steve; I did it when I was alone. I did it because there was something about that moment, when I strolled out of a store, the album hidden, that thrilled me—not so much the possession of the thing itself, but the fact that no one knew what I had done. It was this sabotage that appealed to me, the fact that at just the right moment, when no one was looking, I could take something I had no right to, and thereby disturb the universe in however slight a way only I would know. After years of ugly scenes with my father, here was one way I could control the world.

One evening, after school, I rode with my parents to Lawrenceville, and there I went into a drugstore and stole two albums. My father had parked in front of the Ben Franklin store, where my mother had gone, and when I got back to the car, he and I sat there a moment in silence. I sat in the backseat, and he kept staring at me in his rearview mirror. I tried to think about the field behind our house where the high school track team worked out. They left the high jump standards there, and I liked to see how high I could leap.

Then my father asked me what I was hiding under my coat.

"Nothing," I told him. "There's nothing under my coat."

I was wearing a poplin jacket, and my hands were in the pockets, poofing out the front so no one could see the square corners of the record albums.

"I saw you come out of the drugstore." My father turned so he could look me squarely in the eyes. "And you went around the corner. Why did you go around the corner instead of coming straight back to the car?"

I don't remember exactly how I answered, but I'm sure it was with a feeble lie, something about going around the corner to see whether the public library was open, perhaps. Lies came naturally to me in those days, as I suppose they do to anyone whose life has shifted and slid over into a realm where there are secrets to protect.

My father banged his hooks together the way a prizefighter might tap his gloves before wading out into the middle of the ring to meet his opponent. When I heard the steel clang together, I somehow sensed that I was caught. I may have even been thankful. I lifted the hem of my coat and let the record albums slide out onto my lap.

When my mother came back from the Ben Franklin store, my father told her what I had done. The record albums were there as proof—one by Jimi Hendrix and one by Janis Joplin—and my father was red in the face with rage. My mother, I could tell, was mostly disappointed. She said, "Oh, Lee," her voice tired and flat.

She took me into the drug store, record albums in hand. She made me step up to the counter where the clerk, a pleasant woman wearing a blue smock, was working.

"Tell her," my mother said. "Go on. Tell her what you've done."

Years before, she had taken her father's whiskey bottles and set them on the front steps in hopes that she would shame him into quitting drinking. Like then, she must have been thinking, when she demanded I confess my crime to the clerk, that sometimes you had to give up on the people you loved in order to save them.

I laid the albums on the counter. "I stole these," I said, and I remember that my voice was very soft.

The woman in the blue smock didn't seem to know what to do, and I was sorry for putting her in that predicament.

"Do whatever you have to," my mother said to the clerk.

"You won't do this again, will you?" the clerk said to me.

"No, ma'am," I said as politely as I could, and that was the end of that.

Or so I thought.

When my mother and I got back to the car, my father started going on about his son being a "goddamn thief." He wanted to know what else I had stolen, from whom, and how long it had been going on. "I've had my eye on you," he said. "You'll end up in Vandalia at the state pen. Bread and water, mister."

My mother tried to calm him. "Roy," she said. "Please. Let's go home."

But he wouldn't have any of that. "I don't want to be in the same house with a thief," he said. "He'll rob me blind. Won't you, Mr. Thief? Hell, he might even cut our throats some night when we're sleeping."

The more despicable the picture he painted of me, the more angry I became. I wasn't the person he was describing, but I knew, at that moment, there was no way I could convince him of that. He was determined to dole out the punishment the clerk had refused, to make me feel lost and irredeemable.

I hated my father for making me feel that way. "Shut up," I said to him, but he wouldn't stop. All I wanted was for him to start the car and drive us home, but he wouldn't. I started to feel trapped in that moment forever, and that's when I said, out of desperation, "Shut up, or I'll kill you."

It was the worst possible thing I could have said. Any chance that my father might calm down and drive us home vanished. He really started giving it to me, then, going on about his son the murderer. "I'm afraid to drive home," he said. "I'm afraid Mr. Murderer will choke me from behind. Maybe he's even got a gun or a knife."

"Then what are you going to do?" my mother said.

"I'm going down to Ruth and Don's," he told her. "I'm going to get someone to protect me."

Since we had moved back from Oak Forest, my aunts, Ruth and Lucille, had forgiven my father for leaving. They came to our house often, and we went to theirs to visit or to play cards. Each New Year's Eve everyone gathered for a supper of oyster soup.

Ruth and Don still lived in the rented bungalow on the west end of town near the Texaco oil refinery. Roger could still recite the significant dates in our family's history, and it was the thought of having my crimes announced in his presence, knowing he would remember them forever, that mortified me more than anything else.

All the way to their house, I tried to convince my father to turn around. I cajoled, I pleaded, I threatened, but nothing would deter him, not even my mother's quiet assurances that everything would be all right. "Roy," she said, "you don't want to bother Ruth and Don with this."

For years, my mother had dressed my father, bathed him, shaved him, helped him use the bathroom. She had given so much to him, and that night she only had one simple request: that we go home and keep what had happened to ourselves. But my father insisted on telling this story. Could it have been that all along he had wanted an excuse to reveal our troubled lives to someone so we would be shamed into changing them for good?

At Ruth and Don's, I wouldn't get out of the car. I was too humiliated. I heard my father's voice rising in the bungalow. "A thief," he said. "A thief. You tell me what to do."

Roger came out to the car, and talked to me in a soothing voice. "Do you want me to get Snap?" he said. "Do you want to see him fetch rocks? Or maybe you want to pitch some horseshoes. I could set up the stakes."

I couldn't face him. I curled up in the corner, my face hidden behind my arm, the way criminals do when they know they're on camera, and finally he went back into the house.

"He said he'd kill me," my father said. "Can you imagine that? My son."

There was a long time when I didn't hear anything from the house. Then the back door opened, and someone started walking across the gravel drive to our car. It was Aunt Ruth. She opened the car door, and got into the back seat with me. This was the woman who had saved her son from fever by giving him alcohol baths. She laid her hand on my back and started rubbing it. "Honey, you didn't say those things, did you? Surely, you didn't."

And all I could do was nod my head, admitting that what my father had told her was true.

When I was in the eighth grade, I played Juror #3 in a class production of *Twelve Angry Men*. It's the Lee J. Cobb role, the juror who's convinced that the defendant is guilty and has no patience with the reasonable arguments of the Henry Fonda character. I got to do a lot of finger pointing and table pounding, and in the end, nearly in tears, I got to shout, "All right," as I finally changed my vote to not guilty. After the performance, Mrs. Albiero had said to my mother, "I couldn't believe that was Lee. I had no idea he had that in him."

But it was me as it was that night when Ruth and Don and Roger agreed to accompany us to our home. As I recall, we all rode in our car, and later my father drove them back to their house. By the time we got to Sumner, he had started to calm down. At our house, he showed Ruth and Don and Roger our garden, anxious to talk of turnips and squash and pumpkins.

I left them there and went to the field behind our house and set up the high jump bar. For a long time, I threw myself over it, eager for the feeling of my body in the air, poised above the bar, not knowing whether I had enough lift to make it over. I could hear my parents talking to Ruth and Don and Roger in the garden. I could see them there, disappearing in the dusk, their voices faint echoes in the still night.

My grief at that moment was a misery unlike any I had ever felt. Its mix of yearning, of regret and desire, was as close as I would ever come to understanding my father and the rage that must have moved into him as he stood in that cornfield, his hands and the way he had always known himself about to be lost forever. I felt the cool autumn air and thought of how he had waited for someone to find him. Now it was as if I, too, had slipped away into some distant world where I couldn't touch the people I loved. I couldn't call to them. I couldn't tell them who I was.

Perhaps somewhere deep inside me in a place I couldn't reach, I wanted to corrupt the delight my parents had been able to manage in our new home, a pleasure even I couldn't resist enjoying while at the same time resenting it. How badly I wanted us to be happy, but each sweet, pure moment held within it the reminder of how cruel both my father and I had been. What I wanted more than anything was for him to acknowledge his part in the mistakes we had made. Not once, after all the times he had whipped me, after all the screaming, cursing fights, had he told me he was sorry. Always, I was the one who eventually apologized for my behavior. His response was usually a final jab in my direction. "From now on," he said to me once after he had caught me stealing, "you'd better watch your step. If you don't, I'll have the law throw you in jail. And you know what I'll tell them? 'Throw away the key.' "

At times, I sought comfort from my mother. "He hates me," I said once.

"No, he doesn't hate you," she said. "He loves you. He just gets so mad."

She was happier now that she was away from teaching and back in the part of the country where she felt at home. She had her flowers and her garden, and she was close to her mother and her brother and sister. She knew the signs here: the skeins of geese vee-ing across the evening sky promised that winter would soon arrive, frost clinging to the trees late in the morning predicted snow, quail gathered in the road toward dusk meant rain. She knew the customs: the angel-food cakes baked for Sunday dinners, the meat loafs carried into homes after someone had died, the garden vegetables shared with neighbors, the polite purchase of a plastic salt and pepper shaker at a Tupperware party, a practical wedding gift of towels or pillowcases or casserole dishes. And she knew the language: "I swan," "He's as poor as Job's turkey," "I did three rubbings of clothes today," "I got to wash my head." Like my father, she had come back to a more comfortable notion of herself. He was a farmer again. He bought a new pickup truck, a new tractor, a self-propelled combine. He knew again the smells of freshly plowed earth and diesel fuel and fertilizer. I remember one evening in summer standing with him at the edge of our wheat field. He asked me to pick a head of wheat, rub out the kernels, and put them in his mouth so he could see whether the crop was ready to harvest. I felt his tongue on my fingers, so intimate, and I thought of the summer my mother had gone back to the university, and I had dressed him and bathed him. I put some of the kernels into my own mouth. Now I see us, there in the golden wheat, the sun setting red in the sky, both of us chewing the grain, and I think, it should have been enough, this communion; it should have been enough to forgive every sharp word or violent lash that had preceded it.

But it wasn't. The truth is I couldn't forgive my father, couldn't forgive myself. I resented the fact that they had reclaimed their lives at a time when I had no idea what mine would be. Their futures seemed so certain, so settled; mine was anyone's guess.

"If he loves me, why's he so mean?" I asked my mother.

"We all have to try to be better," she said.

And I thought that was true. But by then I was bent on undermining this opportunity we had to heal ourselves and become whole, and, as the days went by that autumn and winter and on into spring, I slipped further and further away from my parents and their hope that, finally, we were at peace.

One night, I stole our car. It was late, and my parents were in bed, the house dark like all the other houses on our street. My father and I had argued earlier in the evening about the length of my hair. Now that basketball season was over, I had let it grow, and my father had insisted, on this evening, that I get it cut.

"No," I said. "I'm not going to."

We were sitting in the dining room, that also doubled as our family room. My father was kicked back in his recliner, the evening newspaper spread over his lap. My mother was in my Grandma Martin's rocking chair trying to sew a button on the cuff of one of my father's work shirts. The lamps were on, and the door was open to our porch. I could hear June bugs batting against the screen. I imagined someone strolling by catching a glimpse of me lying on the floor leafing through a *Tiger Beat* magazine, and my mother squinting as she tried to thread her needle. Over time, the points of my father's hooks tore holes in his shirt cuffs, and it was hard for her to find a decent patch of cloth where she could attach the button.

"Now listen, mister," my father said. "You're going to do what I say."

I turned to my mother for help. "Mom," I said. "Make him leave me alone."

She was a clumsy seamstress, and, when she sewed, it took all her concentration. "I'm not going to argue." She poked the needle through one of the button holes and into the shirt cuff. "This is between the two of you."

"You're damn right it's between us." My father pushed down the lever of the recliner, and the newspaper slid to the floor as he sat up. It fell across my legs, and I kicked at it, tearing it in the process. "Well, that's just fine," he said. "Now we've got a little tantrum going. You can fuss and whine and cry for Mommy all you want, but here's the fact: if you don't get a haircut tomorrow, I'll hold you down and cut it myself."

"I'd like to see you try."

"You don't think I can do it?"

"I won't let you do it."

"All right, missy. We'll see."

I got up from the floor and stormed into my room. I put *Woodstock*, an album I had stolen, on my stereo. I played Country Joe McDonald's *Fish Cheer*, the song where he gets the audience to spell out "fuck," and then chant it. It was the first time I had played it loud enough for my parents to hear it.

My father came into my room, his face red with anger. "What kind of garbage is that? I want you to turn that goddamn thing off."

I wouldn't look at him. I lay on my bed, staring up at the ceiling.

"You're getting too big for your britches." He stomped over to my stereo. "You need someone to take you down a notch or two."

He knocked the tone arm off the record with his hook. I heard the needle scratch across the grooves.

"Goddamn you." I jumped up from my bed. "You had no right to do that. That's mine."

He turned and pointed his hook at me. "Don't you talk to me like that. I won't stand for it."

I was rushing toward him, angrier than I had ever been. "Get out," I was saying, and then I was pushing at him, trying to shove him out of my room.

He barred his arm across my chest and backed me against the wall. He was strong, his shoulders powerful from all the effort it took to open his hooks. He pressed one of those hooks into my throat. I could smell the steel. I could feel the air closing off in my windpipe, and for a terrifying moment, I was convinced that he might kill me.

Then my mother was shouting at him, one of the few times I can ever recall her raising her voice. "Roy, Roy," she was saying. "Let him go."

He did. He backed away from me, a frightened look on his face as if he had no idea how our lives could ever get back on track after this. I was crying, and one more time, I shouted, "Get out," my voice hoarse, and my parents left my room without a word of protest, stunned, I believe, by what had just happened there.

I lay on my bed and cried and cried, convinced that the rest of my days in that house would be filled with similar scenes. "Stubborn," my mother had said once about my father and me. "You're both just so stubborn." I heard her, in their bedroom, getting my father ready for bed. The points of his hooks scraped the floor as she hung them by their harness over a chair back. I heard the two of them settling into bed, and then the silence insulted me. How could we go through something as vile as we just had and then go off to bed as if nothing out of the ordinary had happened?

Moonlight was shining in through my window, and I could hear a freight train passing through town on the tracks north of our house. I listened to the long, mournful whistle, and thought, as I often did, of what it would be like to someday hide myself away in one of those cars and let the train take me away from my father.

I stepped out into the dining room and saw the keys to his car lying on the table. I picked them up and went to the doorway of my parents' bedroom. I could see my father lying on his back, his white T-shirt stretched across his belly. My mother lay on her side next to him, her gown in loose folds along her legs.

"I'm leaving," I said, and my voice, after so much silence, seemed loud in the dark house. "I'm taking the car."

Of course I wanted them to stop me or I never would have announced my intentions. I would have just gone. I stood there in the dark and waited for their response. Finally, my father spoke. "Did you hear what he said?" he asked my mother.

"I heard him," she said.

There was another long silence, which spooked me, because I had never known my father to be cautious and measured.

Finally, he said, again to my mother, "What do you think we should do?"

He had never left it to her to decide any issue between us, and, even though I had always hoped for her help whenever he had whipped me, I found myself feeling sorry for her because I sensed that so much depended on what she said next, this kind, meek woman who had never been able to discipline the pupils in her classroom.

"We wish you wouldn't," she said, and her voice was so low that I had to lean into the room to hear it. "You don't have your driver's license, and it's probably not a smart thing to do. What do you think?"

At first, I didn't realize she was asking me. I thought she was talking to my father, and his silence made me think about what my life would be like if he were to die and leave only my mother and me in this house. I could see that I would constantly disappoint her, as I surely had countless times. My shame was so great at that moment that I couldn't bear the thought of waking the next morning and coming out of my room to face my parents. Perhaps, they were hoping that cool heads would keep me from doing anything foolish, but, on the contrary, their hesitancy only sent me out into the night, full of anguish.

I started my father's car and gunned the engine. I believed that no one, least of all my parents, loved me. They were willing to let me go away from them. I thought of the day of the Kiwanis Christmas cartoons when I was five and swore I was lost. Then my father had found me. Now he was lying in bed in a house that was as dark—that seemed as peaceful—as any other house in the neighborhood. I kept waiting for a light to come on, for a door to open so my mother or father could call out to me. If they had, I surely would have stayed. But they didn't, and I had no choice but to back the car out into the street, to take off with a roar, tires screaming on the asphalt.

I drove as far as Steve Vernon's, where I parked along the street. His house was a box house with a stone slab outside the front door where his mother often sat in the evenings, smoking Salem cigarettes and flipping the butts out into the shaggy grass. Steve's room was at the rear of the house. I slipped in behind the shrubs and tapped on his window.

He was watching Johnny Carson on the television he had bought with his corn detassling money. I could see the dim glow of the screen spreading out over the bed where Steve lay, pressing the button on his stiletto knife that released the blade. He had found it on the street one day and had made it his prize possession, though he wasn't, by any means, a violent person. He was simply a free-spirited boy who was attracted to anything that was distinctive and entertaining: rock music, an afro, Johnny Carson, anything that would stir up his father, Bill. "Bill's going to shit when he sees this switchblade," he said when he found it. Bill Vernon was a short, wiry man who laid pipe for Marathon Oil. He kept his hair cut close to his head, and there was an oily sheen to his hands and arms. No matter what Steve did, he just called him a knucklehead and let it go at that. The only thing that really got him sore was when Steve stayed up to watch Johnny Carson. Bill had to be on the job early, and he couldn't bear the noise from the television while he was trying to sleep. Now that Steve had his own set, even that problem had been put to rest. Steve seemed to get a kick out of how far he could go to irritate his father, and I envied the good-natured teasing that went on between the two of them.

We were boys who were trying to be men though we had no idea what that meant. Sometimes the things we did surprised us as much as my father's violence had astonished him when he had jabbed his hook into my throat.

"It's all bullshit," I said to Steve that night through his window after I had told him what had happened with my father. "I've got the old man's car. Let's go."

We had talked about it before, how one day we would just disappear. We would steal a car, hitchhike, hop a freight, whatever it took to get the hell out. My own desire for escape sprang from desperation; Steve's, as it turned out, was one more entertaining scenario that caught his fancy for a while and then disappeared.

"Jabbed you in the throat?" he said. "Your dad?"

Behind him, I saw the light from the television screen flicker. The Johnny Carson audience roared with laughter. Suddenly, I felt ridiculous.

"So are you coming?" I said, though by now I was losing my nerve for this scheme.

"Nah," he said. "I got to mow the yard tomorrow."

I went back to my house. What else could I do, really, now that Steve had refused me? I knew I lacked the courage to set out on my own. So I went back.

Since then, I've often wondered what would have happened had I driven out to the highway and tried to run. It would have been all right for a while, I think, driving through the quiet night, the stars bright in the sky, the dash lights glowing as they had the night my father had first driven us to Oak Forest. Maybe I would have tried to have gone there, where people still knew me. Maybe I thought that was where my rightful life should have been taking place. Or, and this is more likely, a state trooper would have spotted me somewhere, and taken me home, and then what would have happened? Would my parents have given up on me? Pressed charges for stealing the car? Would I have ended up in reform school, or, worse yet, the state prison at Vandalia? Would my father have told the warden to "throw away the key"?

Later, I pulled into our drive and shut off my father's car, I sat there a good while, trying to summon up the courage to go into our house, and, by doing so, to admit that I had been wrong to try to leave.

My parents were still in bed. I threw the car keys on the dining table. They landed in the glass ashtray that had belonged to my Grandpa Read, the one who had left the lighters and pipe cleaners and playing cards in the library table drawer my grandmother tried to keep sealed from me as if it were Pandora's box.

"I'm back," I said, and for a good while there was no answer. An odd feeling came over me, then, and like the day I had seen David Sidebottom on the playground, a shiver went down my neck. Just for a moment, before I heard them shifting in their bed, I imagined that, while I had been gone, my mother and father had dressed, packed their suitcases, backed my father's truck out of the garage, and escaped the misery I had brought into their lives.

My mother finally came out of their bedroom. She wasn't wearing her glasses or her dentures, and she seemed more defenseless than she had when she had shouted at my father and told him to let me go. Her arms were bare in her sleeveless gown, and she had them crossed over her chest as if she were freezing though the night was close and warm.

"Is he mad?" I asked her, glancing over her shoulder to their bedroom where I knew my father lay.

"Maybe a little," she said, "but I think he's more hurt than anything. And scared. We're both scared. For you. We don't want to lose you."

"I'm all right." It pained me to see how frail she looked with her eyes so exposed and her mouth all caved in. She looked like my Grandma Read, who, when she stayed with us, shuffled to the bathroom in the middle of the night with a flashlight, casting a beam past my bedroom as if she were a burglar. I was thankful that she hadn't been staying with us on this night. "I'm just tired of him telling me what to do," I said.

"He's your father. He cares about you."

"Is that why he tried to choke me?"

My mother's voice broke as if the air had closed off in her own throat. "Oh, Lee. When you were born, he bragged and bragged. I've never seen someone so proud." I thought of my father in their bedroom, listening to us talk, and for a moment, it was as if he himself had said this to me. I felt an odd mix of embarrassment and guilt and joy. "I know sometimes things can seem horrible," my mother said, "but each new day we can make another start."

I wanted to believe that. "I'll get my hair cut," I said.

She nodded. "That's good."

I imagined my mother and father lying in the dark, letting me drive away from them. "What would you have done?" I said, "if I hadn't come back?"

"We would have called the police." My mother's voice was even and gentle. "We would have told them you were out there."

TEN

One night a year later, when I finally turned sixteen, my father got out of bed, came into the living room, and fell to the floor. He was a big man, and from my own bed, I heard the noise and felt the house shake, and my mother call out, "Roy, Roy, my word."

She switched on a light, and it was vicious, the way light always is in the middle of the night in a house where all has been dark. My father lay on the floor in his T-shirt and boxer shorts. He lay on his back, as if pressed down by the mound of his belly. His stumps stuck out to his sides, short and useless, as if they were flippers and not arms at all.

I was frantic. My father was fifty-eight at the time, a diabetic, and though I had spent a good portion of my teen years despising him, my biggest fear was always that one day, before we could resolve the hostility between us, he would die. "Call the ambulance," I kept saying to my mother. "We should call the ambulance."

She got down on her knees beside my father, the way I had seen her kneel by her bed each night to say her prayers, and she touched him on the arm at the crook of his elbow. The loose folds of her white gown lay in swirls around her, and I thought of the painting that hung above our couch: Jesus kneeling at the rock in the Garden of Gethsemane on the night that Judas would betray him.

"Roy," my mother said, and he groaned. His eyes opened, and she again said, "Roy. Roy, do you want to go to the hospital?"

He blinked his eyes, and I imagined how harsh the light must have seemed to him. "No," he said. "No, I just got dizzy for a while."

"Can you sit up?" she asked.

"I'm all right," he told her.

He tried to lever himself up with his stumps, but it was a difficult chore. My mother turned to me. "Lee," she said. "Help your father."

How odd it felt to be standing over him. I took him under one arm and strained against the burden of his weight, raised up his body. For a moment, we stood there, not moving, not speaking. It was the first time in years that we had touched without anger, and when I finally started to lead him back to bed, our steps were slow and halting as if we were just then learning how to walk.

For some time, I had been inching closer and closer to the point where I would be lost forever. I was a shoplifter, a vandal, an arsonist, a burglar. Steve Vernon and I had figured out the one window always left unlocked on the first floor of the high school, a window conveniently hidden in the shadows of an alcove accessed via a rear alley, and on Saturday nights we pushed open the window and climbed through and spent hours roaming the halls, drinking Cokes in the faculty lounge, scuffing across the gym floor in our boots, stacking lockers so books would come tumbling out when someone opened them.

Our town was a town of alleys. One ran the length of each block, a swath of cinders over hard-packed dirt that skirted the back lots of people's properties. These alleys became our preferred routes as we slinked through the night, sticking to the shadows, waiting for our restlessness to meet some opportunity for mischief.

There was a retired Latin teacher who kept a compost pile of leaves in a wire cage that circled the trunk of a maple tree in her back yard. We saw it one night as we were passing through her alley, and a few days later, I devised a plan. That evening, my friends and I sat in an abandoned house back in a weedy lot on the outskirts of town, and I broke off two match sticks and stuck the heads into a cigarette, one on each side, high up next to the filter. I lit the cigarette, laid it on the floor, and waited. It took twenty minutes for the cigarette to burn down to the match heads and ignite them. "Twenty minutes," I told my friends. "Poof! By that time, we're gone."

It strikes me now that this way of thinking, the anticipation of being in another place when trouble comes down and hearing it then on the lips of people you pass among, none of them knowing that you were the one, is exactly the logic of the subversive. The thrill of wreaking havoc at a time when you are far removed from it. That's the mindset I had. That's how close I was, in 1972, to becoming ruined beyond return. Though I didn't know it, then, there was a line somewhere, a line I couldn't see, and if I stepped over it, I would be gone, and no one, no matter how much they loved me, would be able to get me back.

Still there were times when the nights could turn me and my friends, punks and miscreants all of us, sweet and shy with wonder. On occasion, we forgot about being criminal, dropped our tough-guy facades, and then we were just kids who felt small in the enormous world. We talked, unashamedly, about God, the war in Vietnam, and death. Were our fates predetermined? If we all ended up in Heaven, would we know one another? If we ended up in hell, did eternity really mean forever?

One night in winter, when the wind was screaming across the barren fields, we climbed into an empty grain wagon and slid down the high, slanted walls, until we were in the bottom, huddled together, warmer, looking up at the sky, the wide expanse of it, bright with stars. The wind's howl was muted, then, and for a long time none of us spoke, awed by the sudden calm that was somehow outside the realm of words. In our homes, our parents waited for us, wondering, I'm sure, what had happened to their sons, recalling how sweet we had been, how innocent, when they had first held us in their arms.

The night my father fell to the floor, and I helped him back to bed, everything between us began to change. Some meanness drained out of him, and out of me. Though I'm not sure that we felt any renewal of affection for each other, we did come to a point of some tolerance, the way strange animals, confined to the same space, eventually tire of fighting for dominance and watch one another with wary eyes.

One Saturday, my father drove us down to our farm so we could hunt rabbits. Snow lay on the fields, and the sky was thick with clouds. Out across the white landscape, chimney smoke curled up from farmhouses, and vapor lights came on in barnyards, their sensors fooled by the dark day.

I have since then read about the cold in Siberia, where temperatures drop so low that human breath freezes and falls to the ground, breaking there with a barely audible tinkling. *Zvyozd*, the Siberians call the phenomenon, the "whispering of the stars." Though it wasn't nearly that cold on the day my father and I hunted rabbits, I imagine now, remembering how little we spoke, that we thought our words were that fragile, that if we said the wrong thing it would crack and fall, and lie in pieces at our feet.

We took measured steps through an abandoned hog lot, overgrown with brush. "Be ready," my father said.

I held my single-shot twenty-gauge at an angle in front of me, waiting to swing the stock up to my shoulder, draw back the hammer with my thumb, line up the sights, and squeeze the trigger—all in an instant.

"Right," I said, and we swept along the perimeter of the lot where the snow had clotted the fence rows.

Then, as we eased down the slope toward the old hog house, a rabbit got up, the white fluff of his tail flashing, and began to run.

"There," my father shouted, and I fired.

The rabbit kept running, starting to curve his path back up the slope toward the ridge of the pond, and I caught a final glimpse of his tail before he disappeared into the brush.

"You didn't lead him," my father said. "You've got to lead him. I told you how to do that. Don't you remember?" He banged his hooks together the way he did whenever he wanted to get the right angle for holding something, and for a moment I thought he meant to take the twenty-gauge from me, but he let his arms drop to his sides. "Don't you listen when I tell you anything?"

"I listen," I said, and my voice was sharp because my poor shooting and his criticism had caused the old heat to blaze up between us, the one that had been smoldering since the night he had fallen.

My father's face was red with the cold, and I could see his jaw muscles working the way they always did when he was fuming. Again, he banged his hooks together and the clanging of the steel echoed across the hog lot. I broke the twenty-gauge, and the spent shell fell to the snow with a hiss.

"They always run in circles," my father finally said in a voice that was quiet yet tight with reined-in fierceness like strands of barbed wire woven and stretched to the point of breaking. "Stay here. Get ready now. I'll run him back around to you."

I slid a new shell into the twenty-gauge and watched my father walk away from me. He swung his arms as he slogged through the snow, and I could tell it was tough going for him as he leaned forward and struggled back up the slope. He levelled off and skirted the ridge of the pond. Then he circled to his left and slipped into a persimmon grove, and I lost sight of him.

It was then, as I stood in the cold alone, that I started to recall how, with a sharp word, he had always been able to make me feel weak and inept. Every time I bollixed a job on the farm—when I couldn't drive a nail in straight, or grease a fitting, or loosen a rusted nut—he said I was a pantywaist. "Can't never did nothing," he said. "Try it again."

Before long, I saw him come out of the persimmon grove and start his circle back down the slope. He kicked his way through the brush, sidled through a briar thicket. Then he was out in the open, no more than twenty feet away, coming straight toward me.

That's when I heard the rabbit rustling through the brush. Then there he was, his fur gray against the snow. I raised my twenty-gauge and pulled back the hammer, and there in my sights was my father, a horrified look on his face, both of us realizing what neither had had the sense to understand—no matter how wide the circle, it was still a bent line and eventually we would meet somewhere along its arc.

My hands were shaking. I knew there had been times, when I had been so furious with him that, given this opportunity, I might have pulled the trigger. I thought of Jack Brian and the night he killed his father, Boyd. The thought scared me to death, made me feel how easy it would be to let rage take me far from common sense. I lowered the twenty-gauge, and my father and I stared across the distance at each other, neither of us saying a word, as the rabbit scurried away, desperate for safe cover.

We went home where my mother was reading her Bible at the dining room table. Weak light filtered in through the windows. It was a habit of hers to never turn on a light until she had to, and when I saw her there, her head bowed, I envied the peace she'd found.

"You're back," she said, and she said it with a sigh, just a trace of disappointment. She got up to help my father off with his coat and boots. She would have to help him change his overalls since the legs were caked with snow. "Did you get anything?"

"No," my father said. He glanced at me, and I lowered my head and stomped my feet on the mat inside the door. "Not a thing. We came up empty. I guess we'll have to sing for our supper."

It was as if we had secretly agreed to keep from my mother the moment when we had faced each other in the hog lot, my father held in the sights of my twenty-gauge, because no matter how ugly we were to each other, the truth was we both loved her dearly and wished, for her sake, that we could be better than we were.

On Sundays, my father and I sometimes went with my mother to church. We went to the Church of Christ and sat on a wooden pew and listened to sermons that, for the most part, told us that if we hadn't accepted Christ as our savior, we were damned to spend eternity in hell. Preachers banged their fists on the pulpit, waved their Bibles in the air, and told us at the Judgment Day there would be much wailing and gnashing of teeth, the cries of the lost cast into the fiery furnace forever.

The plan for salvation was simple. If we, the lost, would only come forward, confess our sins, accept Jesus as our savior, be baptized into Christ, and live a Christian life from then on, we would one day ascend to Heaven.

I can still recall how much I wanted to believe this. Every Sunday, when the preacher issued the invitation and the congregation stood and sang, I felt myself outside them, and one of them was my mother, whom I had never meant to harm. Each Sunday, I thought about stepping out into the aisle and making my way to the front of the church where the preacher waited. "Come home," the congregation sang, even my mother in her quiet, reedy voice. "Ye who are weary come home." I wanted to make those steps, because until I did, there would always be the feeling that I was wicked, closed out from a circle of goodness, and what I hated more than anything was to stand there next to my mother, failing her one more time. In those days, I tried to believe I was still the timid child who had come to my mother in the middle of her life, and that eventually I would survive my father's rage and my own and return to the gentle and good way of living she had tried to show me. But when I was in church and the congregation was waiting for me and those like me to confess their sins, I felt vile and beyond redemption.

It was at these moments, in a union of misfits, that my father and I closed ranks. "Brother Lee," he called me as we drove home after church, mocking the reverential way the congregation members addressed one another.

"Yes, Brother Roy," I said.

"I could use some more of that soda cracker, Brother Lee."

This was in reference to the communion service, to the emblems of Christ's body and blood of which only the congregation's brothers and sisters partook. I suspect we chose to mock this part of the service because that was the moment when the lost were made most visible. The silver communion trays went down our pew, and my mother broke off a small piece of the cracker, drank from a thimble-sized cup. My father, because of his hooks, never touched the trays. I held them only long enough to pass them on. Each Sunday this sign presented itself and what it said to anyone who cared to note it was that my mother was saved while my father and I were lost.

"Right away, Brother Roy. And some grape juice?"

"Outstanding, Brother Lee."

And we went on that way like a bad Mr. Bones vaudeville routine.

But we shut our yaps when we saw my mother sitting there with her hands clasped over her Bible, her head bowed, as if she were ashamed to look at us.

The truth was she had something we both envied, some peace that came from faith. No matter how painful we made her life, she believed that one day, she would have bliss. As a girl, she had suffered through her father's drinking problem, and later, as a young woman, her sister's death to cancer. She had married my father when she was forty-one, and he had lost his hands, throwing her forever into the role of the caretaker. Nothing had shaken her resolve. The one constant in a life filled with loss was her conviction that God would reward her endurance.

All through the riot my father and I had brought into our house, I could remember the times, as a small boy, when I had gone with my mother to the Berryville Church of Christ. In my memory, it was always summer. The windows were propped up with the sawed-off ends of broomsticks, and I could hear the breeze rustling through the oak grove, could feel it falling cool across my face. I could smell the varnish of the pews, the paper of the hymnals, the tang of the grape juice as it passed by me in its goblet. I could hear the flap of paper fans stirring the air, the turning of the tissue-thin pages of Bibles, and most of all I could hear the voices rising in song—*Bringing in the Sheaves, In the Sweet By and By, When the Roll Is Called Up Yonder*—and the most bittersweet memory was the way the singing sounded from outside the church on the rare occasions I would get fussy and my mother would have to take me outside.

"Do you want to go home?" she would ask.

I would listen to the singing, such a sweet murmur, yet so distant, like the babble of a brook hidden somewhere in a dark forest.

"No," I would tell her.

"All right then, mister. Straighten up."

On a Sunday afternoon, a few weeks after my father and I had gone rabbit hunting, I told my mother I wanted to join the church. It could be done, she said, at that evening's service. In fact, we would get there early, and she would tell the preacher what I intended. In that way, though she didn't say this, my intent would be made law, and I would be less likely to change my mind when it came time to step out into the aisle. Saying it in advance would make it so.

"We'll need to take a towel," she told me. We were sitting in the living room, my mother in her chair, and I on the ottoman at her feet. "And a change of clothes."

"Clothes?" I said.

She nodded. "To wear for the baptizing. Something old, but not too shabby."

I asked her where I would be baptized since the Church of Christ had no baptistery and it was winter now and too cold to use a pond. She told me that one of the elders would call the Church of Christ in Olney, and after our service was over, we would go there to use their baptistery.

My father was napping in the bedroom, and my mother and I spoke in quiet voices, nearly whispers, as if we were plotting a conspiracy. Outside, the sky was dark with clouds. Our storm windows rattled in their frames.

"What's Dad going to say?" I finally asked.

"This isn't about him," my mother said. "This is you."

She told him when he woke from his nap. I heard them in the bedroom, and behind the closed door their voices were murmurs. My mother spoke for a good while, and though I couldn't hear what she was saying, I suspected that she was making it clear to my father that this decision I had made was what she had hoped for all along and now what she expected from him was his coop-eration. If he dared say anything that might make me change my mind, if he made light the way he and I had done so many times on our drives home from church . . .

My mother's voice went on and on, and I could imagine my fa-ther sitting on the edge of the bed, his head hanging down, his bare stumps resting on his belly, the posture I remembered from the night when he had fallen and I had helped him. When he fi-nally spoke, it was only a few words, and when he came out into the living room, he didn't look at me. He stood at the window. "Looks like snow," he finally said.

At church, when it came time for the invitation, the congrega-tion sang *Softly and Tenderly*, and when I came forward, the preacher, a Brother Toliver, shook my hand, and led me to the front pew where I sat until the singing had finished. Then he asked me whether I had come to repent of my sins, whether I believed in Jesus Christ and was prepared to be buried with him in baptism and to rise and walk in a new life. And I said that I was.

Then I stood and faced the congregation, and as they sang an-other song, the members circled by me and extended to me the right hand of fellowship, welcoming me to their fold. Some of them mumbled words of encouragement. They congratulated me. They told me I had done well. They called me their brother. When it was my mother's turn, she merely took my hand, held it a bit longer than the others had, gazed up at me with damp eyes. My fa-ther waited at the back of the church, the only one there, not per-mitted to come forward and greet me.

In a few minutes, we would drive to Olney, and Brother Toliver would lead me down into the baptistery and announce that he was baptizing me in the name of the Father, and of the Son, and of the Holy Ghost. Then he would cover my mouth and nose with his handkerchief and tip me back into the water.

But for a while longer, I stood at the front of the church as the members circled past me. Between each of them, as if I were spinning on a merry-go-round, I caught a glimpse of my father. He was making his way to the end of the pew, and glimpsing him in the spaces between the passersby, I got the sense that I was watching the halting motions of a flipbook or the frames of film passing through a kinetoscope. With each peek, he had moved closer to the aisle, and I felt rising in me a great hope that what he had decided was that he would come to the front of the church and tell Brother Toliver that he, too, wanted to be saved. Then, I saw him step into the aisle, turn, and start walking to the church doors. Each time I saw him, he had moved farther away from me.

I feared that he would leave, drive off into the night and never return. Then my mother and I stepped outside the church, where, by this time, snow had started to fall. Our car was running. Clouds of exhaust fogged up behind it. The wipers were clearing the snow from the windshield. Though I couldn't see my father, I knew that he was there, somewhere in the dark. I wanted to tell him I was sorry, but I knew I wouldn't. I couldn't. He was my father. He had his own guilt to bear.

ELEVEN

So many nights that winter, I stood at our door and watched the snow slant down past the streetlights' globes. The wind howled in our stovepipe. The storm windows rattled in their frames. The snow blew across our front porch, filled in our driveway, lay in drifts and swirls across our lawn. Our roof timbers groaned and popped, and sometimes ice slid over our eaves and came down with a crash in my mother's flower beds.

"You'd think the world was ending," she said one night. She was standing in front of our stove, warming herself. "Mercy, it gives me the shivers."

I didn't mind the snow. I liked the idea of my mother and father and me sealed away safely in our house while the storm raged out-side. I liked the flare of the gas stoves, the rush of hot air, the warmth of my Grandma Martin's quilt wrapped around me. When we turned off our lights for the night, the snow cover cast a soft glow across the beds where we slept. Each morning, as I dressed for school, my father told me to bundle up because it wasn't fit to be out. He bought me a pair of insulated boots made of green rubber and insisted that I wear them to school. I thought they looked old-fashioned and hickish, something a pig farmer would wear to slop through his pens, and I said so.

"You'll be glad for them," my father said, "out there in that snow."

And, secretly, I was glad, happy that he had bought the boots for me. I took his gift as a sign that he forgave me everything—the trouble I had fallen into, and the fact that I had been baptized and left him the only one in our family who was lost.

From time to time, his diabetes discouraged him. Fortunately, the disease wasn't serious enough to require insulin injections; instead, his blood sugar could be controlled with an oral medication and a more prudent diet. He had always eaten with abandon: fried foods, desserts, sweet tea. He had a special affinity for Pepsi-Colas, butter pecan ice cream, deep-fried mushrooms, rhubarb pie, vanilla milkshakes. Food had always been one of his true pleasures in life. Now he had to make do with diet soda pops, artificial sweeteners that left a bitter aftertaste in his mouth, and sugarless chewing gum he said he enjoyed about as much as chomping on paraffin. I thought of how he loved, each Christmas, to bring home bags and bags of candy, and how, in the summer when we came back into town from a day's work on the farm, he liked to stop at the drugstore and send me in for ice cream drumsticks. Some of the most pleasant times I had ever spent with him involved food—the watermelons we ate late at night in the hot summers; the Pepsis we drank at Ed White's store; the slabs of blackberry cobbler we poured cream over on Sundays. And though I was sad to think moments such as those might be rare now that my father was ill, I noticed in his melancholy a submission to the unexpected turns a life could take that I imagined might make things easier for all of us. He often sat for long periods of time, not saying a word, and when he finally spoke, it was with a sigh as if the weight of the world were on him. "What can a fella eat?" he would say with regularity. "It's a dirty trick. I can tell you that."

My mother accommodated him by learning how to cook with artificial sweetners. She bought diabetic candy at the grocery store, used a kitchen scale to ration his servings at meals. She seemed to enjoy the fact that she was looking out for him. "Oh, this won't be so bad," she told him. "You'll see."

Where would we have been without her eternal optimism? Though she had stood by, silent, while my father had whipped me when I was a child, she had at least always believed—and somehow had made me believe—that our lives were worth more than the shabby way we often treated them. She lacked the courage to confront my father's rage or to escape it, but she endured, and by doing so, she slowly began to win the long battle for goodness that was the history of our family.

Not long after I had been baptized, she had gone to work at the nursing home in town. Sometimes she worked on the housecleaning crew; other times, she labored in the laundry or in the kitchen. She did this despite the fact that she often had to work on Sundays. When that was the case, I didn't go to church, preferring to wait until the evening service when she and I went together. We walked the three blocks to the church building, often through the snow and the cold. She wore boots with fake fur fringing the tops, or, if the snow was light, clear, plastic rain booties that slipped over her shoes and buttoned at her ankles. She had a woolen scarf with a tartan design of black and green, and black woolen gloves with a row of three buttons at each wrist. She wore a brooch pinned to her coat and carried a pocketbook that held, among other things, cough drops, an embroidered handkerchief, and a dollar bill, already neatly folded for the offering.

When she died in 1988, she left behind a small black purse with a gold snap and a strap just the right length for dangling daintily from her wrist. Inside was a pair of navy blue gloves that had tiny white beads sewn along the cuffs, a handkerchief with a map of Wisconsin on it, a hair brush, and a wallet. The wallet was a billfold with a coin purse inside, a long pocket for cash, and a compartment of plastic sheaths for photographs and documents. It was a practical wallet, so unlike the ones I had often given her at Christmas and Mother's Day, more feminine models with mirrors inside and places for lipsticks and checkbooks and ballpoint pens. She had always made a fuss over those wallets, but now I'm sure they never really suited her. She never thought of herself as the sort of woman—young and stylish—who would carry such a thing.

Sometimes, on those Sunday nights when we walked to church, she took my arm so if she were to slip on the snow-packed side-walk, I would be there to steady her. I liked being her escort through the dark and the cold, stepping finally into the light and the warmth of the church. I liked sitting next to her during the service and holding the communion tray between us as we both sipped from the delicate glasses.

What went through my father's head while we were gone, I can't say. All I know is that when we were finally back in the house, he seemed glad to have us there. He turned off the television he had been watching and asked my mother to pop some corn and peel some apples. We sat at our kitchen table; he ate his popcorn from a bowl with a spoon. Who had been in church, he wanted to know. And how was Mrs. Byram's arthritis? And Mr. Wilig's gout?

"If you're so curious," my mother said one night, "why don't you come along next time and find out for yourself?"

"Oh, I don't imagine anyone wants to see me."

"Brother Toliver asked about you."

"What did you tell him?"

"I told him you were at home watching some shoot-em-up on TV."

"I bet he liked that. What'd he say? That I was a heathen?"

"He said to tell you hello. That's all."

Luther Toliver was the only minister my father had dealt with who didn't seem particularly interested in saving his soul. Mr. Toliver had been a housepainter most of his life. He was a working man instead of a "pencil pusher," and I imagine that was why my father found him likeable. On the occasions when my father went to church, he lingered in the foyer after the service to talk with Mr. Toliver about the weather and what it might mean for the spring planting. Mr. Toliver was a lanky man with an easy laugh, and he often patted my father on his back and asked him how he was doing. "Can't complain," my father usually said.

And it was true that since my baptism he had grumbled less. Outside the moments when he moaned about having to watch his diet, he was agreeable. Now that winter had come, and there was little that demanded his worry on the farm, he was more pleasant. I came home at lunch and warmed soup for us and made lunch meat sandwiches, and we chatted for twenty minutes or so before I went back to school. He spent his afternoons loafing at the barber shop or the pool hall or the grain elevator. Often he walked uptown, and toward evening, when my mother had started our supper, I stood at our side window and watched up the street, anxious to see him coming down the sidewalk. I feared, the later and later it got, that some misfortune had come to him, the way it had the night he had fallen. Then I would see him. I would recognize his sheepskin coat with the fleece collar, his wool cap with the ear tabs pulled down, the steel of his hooks glinting as he passed beneath the streetlights. When he came in our house, the warm air steamed up his eyeglasses, and until I helped him take them off, he was blind. I helped him out of his coat and his boots, and he went into the kitchen where he usually told my mother and me a funny story he had heard uptown. No matter how painfully he felt the circumstances of his life he always found some way to enjoy it.

Sometimes the smallest things could please him—a cup of hot tea, a slice of longhorn cheese, a new flannel shirt, the call of a mourning dove, the taste of wheat kernels when they were full and ripe. He was always, I realize now, a sensualist, driven by appetite and the world of the body. He had no hands with which to touch, but he could taste and hear and smell, and he sought out those things that stimulated his senses: the champagne he became infatuated with when we lived in Oak Forest, the tweed hats, the pint of Old Granddad whiskey he kept hidden in the kitchen cabinet, the sardines he developed a fancy for after he learned he had diabetes, the oyster soup he ate with my aunts and uncles on New Year's Eve, the lush plants in his garden, the apple and peach trees he grew in our backyard.

I only saw him kiss my mother twice: once on her birthday, and once, toward the end of their time together. What went on behind the closed doors of their bedroom, I don't know, but from observing their daily come and go, it was clear that my father was embarrassed by physical affection and rarely granted it himself. If he wanted to "touch" someone, he did it through kindness: the sacks of candy and nuts and fruit he insisted we leave for the Sidebottoms all those years ago, a bushel of apples shared with one of my aunts, the new dresses he insisted my mother buy, the snow he shoveled from Mr. Murray's walk, the one hundred dollars he gave to a family down on their luck. Such benevolence was as much a part of him as was his rage.

Then one day I said to him, "I worry about you."

We were repairing a bed frame. Both of us were sitting on the floor, and my father looked at me as if I were the screw we were having a hard time fitting into the warped, wooden rail—as if he had no idea what to do with me.

"Worry?" he said. "What do you mean? I'm all right. This sugar I've got? It's under control."

"No, not the sugar," I said.

"What then?"

"I wish you would join the church."

Since my baptism, I had thought of what Mr. Browning had suggested to my father the night he and Mr. Laycoax had come to our duplex in Oak Forest, that someday my mother and I might end up in Heaven without my father, and I was convinced that, deep down, he didn't want that to happen. The alternative, of course, was the burning hell so many preachers had depicted, and despite the punishment my father had inflicted on me over the years, I couldn't bear the thought of him cast into a fiery pit for all of eternity. I believed in forgiveness, then, because I, myself, had been redeemed. I knew the feeling of euphoria that came over me the night my father drove us home from my baptism, the sense of well-being this second chance had brought me. I had gone into my mother and father's bedroom, had lain back on this same bed that my father and I were now trying to repair, and asked my mother, "If something happened, and I died tonight, would I go to Heaven?" She told me I would, and I lay there awhile, enchanted with the notion that, just as the scripture promised, someone could put away the old person and rise from the baptismal water a new and blameless creature. I wanted that salvation for my father.

He nudged a hammer toward me. "Knock on the screw with this," he said. "Maybe you can force it in."

I knew I had put him on the spot with my request that he join the church, made him feel as hopeless as I had felt the many times when preachers had issued the invitation. How could I tell him what I felt? That I loved him—all along, even at our worst times, there had been this love. I imagined that he felt it, too, though I could never recall him saying it.

When I tried to hammer the screw into the rail, the wood split, and immediately I thought of all the times I hadn't been able to perform a chore to his liking, and my father had taunted me. This time, he only said, "It's being ornery, isn't it? It doesn't want to co-operate. Go get the electrical tape."

My father was a great patcher and repairer, and the black electrical tape was one of his principal tools. I had seen him use it to mend a radiator hose, a hole in the bed of our old truck, the torn leather of a boot. We used it on this day, to wrap the split in the wood, and then, by some miracle, I got the screw to go in, and the bed was, at least for a time, stable. My father pressed the point of his hook into the floor to brace himself, and then he tried to push himself up. I heard him grunt with the effort. I was standing over him, the way I had the night he had fallen, and I reached out and took his arm. He looked up at me with surprise and shame, and I knew I had embarrassed him.

"Here now," he said. "What do you think you're doing?"

"I'm trying to give you a hand," I said.

He shook free from my grasp. "I'll be all right. I don't need your help."

Not long ago, when I was back in southern Illinois, visiting my wife's family, I went to the library and found, in a newspaper dated Thursday, December 6, 1956, a card of thanks my father had put in the classified section after he had lost his hands.

I want to thank everyone who has helped me in any way, by words of encouragement, with cards, flowers, money and donated labor. Each deed was greatly appreciated.

—Roy Martin

I couldn't help but note that this thank you had appeared almost exactly one month to the day of my father's accident, while another farmer, who had lost a hand on the same day, had placed his note nearly two weeks earlier. Had my father dragged his feet with his own note because he was reluctant to admit that he was now a "handicap," an unfortunate soul who needed, at least for a time, to rely on the kindness of his neighbors? Had his "thank you" been a grudging one, sincere but also resentful? Had my mother, weary of his refusal to do so, composed the note and placed it for him? Of course, I don't have the answers to any of these questions, but when I try to imagine what it was like for him in the weeks that passed after his accident and again after I was baptized, I know that while he was always quick to offer help to others, he was loath to admit it when he needed it himself.

One day, not long after we repaired the bed, we both went uptown for haircuts. There, in the barber shop, a man I didn't know couldn't stop staring at my father's hooks. "Buddy," he said, "it must be hell." He was younger than my father. He was a skinny man with a long neck and a large adam's apple. He had a cigarette in his mouth, and the smoke was curling up past his left eye. He squinted at my father's hooks and shook the newspaper he was reading at them. "Those gizmos," he said. "I can't imagine."

"I do all right," my father said. He was sitting across the room from the man, next to the glass case where the barber kept his creams and tonics. I was in the chair, feeling the tissue paper scratching at my neck and the snippety-snip of the barber's scissors. As always, when someone took notice of my father's hooks, I was uncomfortable. Through the window, I could see the red and white stripes of the barber pole turning, and in the street, the clouds of exhaust fogging out of tailpipes as cars passed. It was almost five o'clock, and the dark would soon be upon us, and people were on their way home.

"I bet you do, buddy," the man said. "But still." He shook his head. "Well, I'll tell you this. I wouldn't want to be in your shoes."

I saw the muscles clench in my father's jaws, the way they had so many times before he had whipped me or we had fought, and I wanted to tell the man to shut up, to read his newspaper and smoke his cigarette and leave my father alone.

But the man wouldn't let up. "How do those gizmos work, anyhow?"

"Why don't you get you a set of your own?" My father stood up. "Then you can figure it out for yourself."

There was anger in my father's voice, and the man heard it. "Whoa, buddy. I didn't mean nothing. I was just gabbing. You know, passing the time. I'm just saying you've got a rough row to hoe."

My father reached up to his shirt pocket, opened his hook, and took out his billfold. He laid it on the glass case and pried it open. Then, he tried to fish out the bills he needed to pay the barber for our haircuts. Normally, I would have been the one to do all of this, but I was still in the chair, my head held firmly between the barber's fingers. "I'll be outside," my father said to me. "I'll warm up the truck."

The man folded his newspaper and let it drop onto the seat next to him. "Hey, buddy." He stood up. "Let me get that for you."

He reached for my father's billfold. My father tried to knock his hand away, and in the process his hook came shut and pinched the man's finger. "Judas Priest," the man said. He was shaking his finger in the air. "You ought to watch those things. You could hurt someone."

I thought of the moment, years before, when my father had

jammed his open hook into the school superintendent's crotch, and started us on the long journey to Oak Forest and back. As I had then, I felt how fragile any truce with my father always was. A wrong word, a suspect look, and everything could fly apart.

With great care and effort, he slid three dollar bills from his billfold and left them on the glass case. He closed the billfold and slipped it back into his shirt pocket. "*You* ought to be more careful," he said to the man. "You shouldn't stick your fingers into something that's not your business."

"I was just trying to do you a good turn, buddy."

"I'm not your buddy," my father said. "I don't even know who you are."

He went to the door and tried to open it, but his hook slipped from the knob. The barber started to go to help him but the skinny man with the adam's apple beat him to the punch. He opened the door for my father, and I felt the cold air sweep across my legs.

"Just to show there's no hard feelings," the man said, and my father, though I suspect he would have preferred anything to accepting the man's kindness, stepped out into the dusk. The man closed the door, and I saw my father, on the sidewalk, turn back, just for an instant, before he went on to his truck.

That night, at supper, he was quiet. "Cat got your tongue?" my mother asked.

"I'm worn out," he told her.

"Are you sick?"

"No, I'm not sick. I'm just tired."

I imagine now that, finally, my father simply grew weary of sustaining the anger that had controlled his life so long. Sixteen years had passed since he had been careless and let his hand slip between the corn picker's rollers. Since then, he had always been on guard, quick to lash out at anyone he suspected of trying to take advantage of him: the superintendent, Leslie Feary; my Aunt Lucille and Aunt Ruth; the various elders and preachers from the church who had tried to save him; me. Over the years, I have lived my own life of anger, and I know it is a hard life to live, not only for those who happen to be in the way of my occasional outbursts of temper, but also for me who fights, always, the inclination to rage handed down from my father. Without my mother's counterbalance of forbearance and compassion, which I also carry with me, I fear I would be lost indeed. Still, there are times when I catch myself lashing out with a sharp word, and I hear my father in my voice, feel him in the set of my jaw, the swinging of my arms, the tightness in my throat. Sometimes, as I do now, he would get so angry he would cry. He would scream until he was hoarse, and his face would be shiny with tears. And I would want to do anything I could to make him stop, to let him know that, no matter the troubles between us, I loved him.

One Sunday evening, a few weeks after the episode with the skinny man at the barber shop, my father said, "It's cold out there. Almost zero." He had been out to read the thermometer on the back of the house. "And the wind's fierce. You'd better not walk to church tonight."

He went out to the car and sat there in the cold, keeping the engine idling so everything would be warm when my mother and I finally joined him. Then he drove us, over streets blanched white with the cold, toward the church. I could see the street signs twisting in the wind, could hear the clatter of tree branches.

Inside the church, the gas furnace was roaring, and we sat close to one another in the pew—my mother and father and I—letting the cold leave us. I sat near the aisle, and my mother sat between my father and me.

It was during the invitation, as we all stood to sing, that I suddenly felt my father pushing past my mother, knocking against me with his hook, as he came out into the aisle. I glanced at my mother, who was still looking down at her hymnal as if nothing out of the ordinary had happened. But there was my father, marching to the front of the church where Luther Toliver was waiting for him. The song we were singing was *Just As I Am*, and my father was moving with the same bluster that had carried him through so much of his life. Even now, at the moment of his repentance, he was stomping ahead with force and purpose, as if he feared that one moment of delay or hesitation might be enough to make him turn back.

I knew the courage it took for my father to make that walk, to confess to the congregation that he was lost. I knew how long my mother must have wished it, must have prayed for it each night when she knelt beside her bed. They would have only nine years left to them after this night, but they would be calmer years, kinder ones. On a Friday evening, in the heat of August, my mother would hear the lawn mower engine suddenly rev, the throttle jerked wide open as my father fell, already dead from a heart attack, the last sound of his leaving the world, a roar to the heavens.

For years, I've imagined what it must have seemed like to my mother's ears when Mr. Murray, who had been working in his garden, came running and shut off the lawnmower. It must have been such a peaceful calm, such a dreadful quiet.

The last thing I ever said to my father was, "Don't work too hard."

By this time, I had married and was living eighty miles away in Evansville, Indiana. My father was sixty-nine years old; my mother seventy-two. We had all survived our lives. I worked for a program that helped disadvantaged young people get into college. My mother had retired from the nursing home and that year, she had tutored a boy who was ill and couldn't go to school. She also taught Sunday school, and my father, when called upon, led prayers in church and did scripture readings. Often, on weekends, my wife and I went to visit, and on Sunday afternoons, if it was summer, my father and mother took us out into their garden to let us choose fruits and vegetables to take home with us. My father was always insistent. "Take this melon," he would say, "and some more of this corn." We gathered beans and tomatoes and squash. "That's enough," I would finally say, but it was never enough for my father who knew we had so much to make up to each other and offered the bounty of all he had cared for and grown as a way of saying he was sorry that so much of our life together had been difficult.

I believe I forgave him completely, and forgave myself, the moment I saw him step into the aisle at church that cold Sunday night.

As he had done so many times when they had been merely talking about the weather and the crops, Luther Toliver patted him on the back. He eased my father down onto his knees, and he knelt beside him, and as we kept singing, he said a quiet prayer of thanksgiving that this one man, my father, had come forward to be saved.

When he was baptized, he went down into the water without his hooks, the weathered flesh of one stump on Luther Toliver's hand that held a folded handkerchief to my father's nose. Later, in a small room behind the baptistery, I took the wet clothes from my father, and when he was naked, I dried him with a towel, marvelling over how white his skin was on his stomach and legs and back—how smooth, as if nothing had ever touched it—when his stumps were leathery and worn, particularly around the scars where the surgeon's saw had violated the flesh, had taken skin and muscle and tendon and bone.

Now I think about my father coming home after the amputation and still being able to feel his hands at the ends of those stumps, the phantom hands that would wake him in the night with imagined pain and send him reaching for the phenobarbital tablets, only to realize that he had no fingers, no hands. How easily our bodies become us, our souls bound to the material, to the joy or grief or pain we feel through our skin. My father had been doomed to years of rage because he lost his hands. For too long, I was full of temper and fear because of the lashes from his belt. But on this cold Sunday night, all of that was changing. Steam rose from my father's body. His white skin turned pink as I rubbed it dry. I helped him into his fresh clothes. I combed his hair.

He was quiet, amazed by it all. "It's funny what a guy can do, isn't it?" he finally said.

I thought of all the marks he had left on me with his belt, all the times we had nearly ruined each other. "Yes," I told him, "it's funny."

Then we went out into the church where my mother was waiting. She was alone in the foyer, her hands in her coat pockets, her pocketbook dangling from her arm. At first glance, I thought she looked unsure of herself, not knowing what she should do. Her head was tipped down so her face was partially hidden, as was common whenever there was too much happening too quickly around her, and she felt overwhelmed. I imagined all the times she had stood like that—in the hospital when my father had lost his hands, in her classroom when her pupils had misbehaved, in our various homes when my father and I had erupted in anger. Her shoulders were rounded, her back starting to stoop, and I imagined that each time my father had whipped me or we had fought, she had taken the lashes and blows into her own body, and they had begun to break her down. Then I noticed the trace of a smile on her lips, and I knew she was content to wait as long as she might have to, confident that, finally, my father and I would find her there, and, together, we would go home.

Acknowledgments

I am deeply indebted to my agent, Phyllis Wender, for her wise counsel and generous advocacy, and to my editor, Laurie Chittenden, who with extraordinary skill and grace has made my work a joyful education.

I am also grateful to Susie Cohen, Sonia Pabley, and Jordan Pitcher for all their efforts on my behalf, and to the editors at the following publications where portions of this book in somewhat different form have appeared: *Crab Orchard Review, Creative Nonfiction, The Georgia Review, The Journal, The Sun,* and *Harper's Magazine.*

The Texas Commission on the Arts and the University of North Texas have favored me during the writing of this book, and my colleagues and students, past and present, have sustained me through all my work. The names of some of the people who play minor roles in this narrative have been changed to protect privacy, and for their brief appearances in my life I am thankful as I am for all my relatives whose heritage I share.

Most of all, I offer my heart to my wife, Deb, my best friend now for nearly twenty-five years, and to Mildred and Harry for their love and support.